chapman

P9-CBD-047

The Pueblo Storyteller

chapman

chapman

The Pueblo Storyteller

DEVELOPMENT OF A FIGURATIVE CERAMIC TRADITION

Barbara A. Babcock

Guy and Doris Monthan

The University of Arizona Press

TUCSON & LONDON

About the Authors

BARBARA BABCOCK began gathering information in 1978 on the history of the figurative tradition in Pueblo Indian ceramics and the art and experience of Helen Cordero. She has published and lectured widely on the development of the Storyteller and its effect on contemporary Pueblo ceramics and culture. She has taught at the University of Texas, Brown University, where she was director of the Pembroke Center for Teaching and Research on Women, and is presently professor of English and Comparative Literature at the University of Arizona. Trained in comparative literature and anthropology at the University of Chicago, Professor Babcock has published widely in folklore, symbolic anthropology, literary criticism, and feminist studies. Most recently, she has co-authored *Daughters of the Desert: Women Anthropologists in the Southwest, 1880–1980* (1988).

GUY AND DORIS MONTHAN, a husband-and-wife, photographer-writer team, have collaborated on books and articles on American Indian art since the late 1960s. Among their publications are the award-winning *Art and Indian Individualists* (1975) and *Nacimientos* (1979), the first book to be devoted solely to the figurative art of Indian potters of the Southwest.

Photographers who have contributed their work to this volume include: J. Bradley Babcock (Color Plate 1), Robert Nugent (Color Plate 8), Glenn Short (Color Plates 2, 3), Dudley Smith (Figure 10), Arthur Taylor (Figure 11), Helga Teiwes (Figure 2), and Ben Wittick (Figure 5). The photographer for Figure 9 is unknown.

All other color plates and black and white photographs are by Guy Monthan.

Fifth printing 1992

THE UNIVERSITY OF ARIZONA PRESS

Copyright © 1986
The Arizona Board of Regents
All Rights Reserved

This book was set in 11/14 ITC Cheltenham Light.
Manufactured in the U.S.A.
⊗ This book is printed on acid-free, archival-quality paper.

Library of Congress Cataloging in Publication Data

Babcock, Barbara A.
  The Pueblo Storyteller.

  Bibliography: p.
  Includes index.
    1. Pueblo Indians — Pottery.   2. Indians of North
America — New Mexico — Pottery.   I. Monthan, Guy.
II. Monthan, Doris.   III. Title.
E99.P9B13   1986   783.3'7   86-4279
ISBN 0-8165-0870-4
ISBN 0-8165-1193-4 pbk.

Contents

Illustrations

Figures

Prehistoric and Historic

Keres Pueblos

The Towa Pueblo of Jemez

Tewa Pueblos

Tiwa Pueblos

Zuni Pueblo

Color Plates

Keres Pueblos

Map

Foreword

The development of the Storyteller figure, so aptly recounted in the pages which follow, is a short course in the making of a tradition. As such, it is a story of individuals, with a cast of characters that crosses cultural boundaries. As the drama unfolds, these people express their own culturally determined biases, conduct their lives in an industrialized society, and respond to both their inner necessities and the exigencies of the marketplace.

A few individuals take center stage. First and foremost there is master potter Helen Cordero of Cochiti Pueblo. Her vision was an inspired one: drawing upon the venerable traditions of the past, aware of the unspoken but, nonetheless, strongly self-evident rules which guide those traditions, she chose to innovate. And — as is often the case for the artist who makes a personal quest, no matter what his or her background or audience — in that innovation she found herself. Helen arrived at pottery making at the time when she had fulfilled most of her duties as a mother, and in her middle age she both sparked a revival of figurative pottery and revolutionized it.

Alexander Girard's influence as a patron and fellow creator (he is himself a renowned designer and architect) must not be diminished. He bought Helen's first Storyteller, and his enthusiasm for her concise and individualistic style had a telling effect on her self-confidence. His suggestion for "improvements" on the Singing Mothers she initially sold him were taken to heart, and the assurance of future purchases by the Girards afforded Helen an artistic freedom rarely enjoyed by her peers. It was no surprise to discover in 1978, when the Girard Collection was donated to the Museum of International Folk Art in Santa Fe, that it contained 684 Cochiti ceramics, nearly all figurative, and nearly all contemporary. Within that group were 55 single and composite figures by Helen Cordero, including a commissioned Nativity scene of 115 pieces.

Yvonne Lange and Sallie Wagner also played leading roles in the development of the Storyteller tradition. In 1972, Dr. Lange, then director of the Museum of International Folk Art, undertook the task of assembling a ground-breaking exhibition entitled "What Is Folk Art?" A portion of this exhibition investigated the various agents of change which affect the evolution of folk-art forms. One section specifically addressed the influence of individuals who, by virtue of their genius or commitment or downright single-mindedness, changed the course of a folk tradition. In planning for this section, the museum enlisted the aid of Sallie Wagner, a long-time collector of American Indian art and herself such an individual, having sparked a revival of Navajo weaving and the use of vegetal dyes in Wide Ruins during the 1930s. On the museum's behalf, Sallie visited her old friend Helen Cordero as well as several of the other Cochiti potters who, by the early 1970s, had also begun to produce Storytellers.

Sallie acquired six examples of these potters' work, along with Helen's, for the exhibition, where they were photographed together (see Figure 11). Some eight years after Helen Cordero had fashioned her very first Storyteller for folk-art collector Girard, this "tradition" still seemed very new, and the work of her followers was still considered merely imitative. By 1986, that photograph seemed like a moment frozen in time, as we found ourselves confronted with a form which had evolved from the inspired vision of one master potter into an artistic and commercial phenomenon of impressive proportions. By the mid-1980s, more than 175 potters throughout New Mexico in a variety of Pueblos had embraced this subject.

In the late 1970s, three people were brought together by their interest in the Storyteller figure. In researching the art and cultural experience of Helen Cordero, Barbara Babcock, a scholar trained in literature and anthropology, turned her attention and insight to a number of questions addressed in the text of the present volume: What are the sources of this figurative tradition? How did the Storyteller develop and how does it fit into this earlier tradition? What is its meaning to the innovator, her followers, her market? These questions probe the very assumptions which underlie our definitions and understanding of ethnic and tourist art. Guy and Doris Monthan, collaborators on numerous publications on American Indian art since the late 1960s, brought years of knowledge and expertise to the project. Their interest in Storytellers grew from work on their 1979 book,

Nacimientos, which dealt with a related aspect of figurative Pueblo ceramics, and they carefully documented biographical and artistic information and prepared the excellent illustrations (both black-and-white photographs and color plates) for this volume.

By joining forces, the three authors contributed and combined many years of research, documentation, and experience in order to produce this fine book. To those of us with a deep interest in traditional and ethnic art, the lack of information about the origins, use, and development of artistic traditions in this field is often a cause for considerable lament. What a pleasure it is, then, to bear witness to a tradition in the making in the pages which follow. For preserving the record, readers of this volume owe a sincere debt of thanks to the authors.

CHARLENE CERNY

Museum of International Folk Art
Santa Fe, New Mexico

Preface

 As a collaborative effort among Barbara Babcock, Guy Monthan, and myself, this book began in June 1979, but its roots go back for several years before that. When Guy and I saw our first Storyteller and met its creator, Helen Cordero, in 1971, we could not have foreseen how many times our paths would cross. Helen and her art were included in our first book, *Art and Indian Individualists* (1975). A few months after its publication, as we began research for our second book, *Nacimientos* (1979), she was again one of the first artists we contacted, and, prior to completion of the book, we were asked to do an article on her for the pottery issue of *American Indian Art* magazine in 1977. About midway through *Nacimientos*, we discovered that most of the artists who made Nativities were also making Storytellers. This development seemed a mandate to do a book on Storytellers, and we were gathering information and taking photographs of them as we went along. (In fact, of the thirty-five Pueblo potters represented in *Nacimientos*, thirty have been included in this book. In reverse manner, more than half of the Storyteller artists included here — many more than we had found in our initial research — have also made Nativities.)

In 1977, Barbara Babcock had her first introduction to the Storyteller, and certainly she could not have imagined the multiple off-shoots which would spring from that first encounter. In that year, while a Weatherhead Scholar at the School of American Research in Santa Fe, she began working with Helen Cordero on "Stories Told in Clay," a book about Helen's art and experience, and in the process, collecting material on the Storyteller phenomenon. At Helen's suggestion, Barbara wrote to us in May 1979, and we arranged to meet in Flagstaff. Since we were all doing research along the same lines, we decided to collaborate on a general survey of Storyteller artists, while Barbara would continue independently with her book on Helen. From 1978 to 1986, Barbara published eight articles and book chapters on Helen Cordero, the Storyteller, and on the history of Cochiti figurative ceramics. Her 1983 *American Indian Art* essay, "Clay Changes: Helen Cordero and the Pueblo Storyteller," served as a preview of this book. She also gave many lectures on the same subjects at museums and universities from Tucson to Groningen, the Netherlands, and Bergen, Norway. In 1981, she was guest curator of "Tales for All Seasons," a major retrospective exhibit of Helen Cordero's work and the Cochiti figurative tradition at the Wheelwright Museum in Santa Fe.

Having already done extensive research on the historic aspects of the theme, Barbara undertook preparation of the text concerning the development of the Storyteller tradition and its place in Pueblo art (Part I of this book), as well as the glossary and bibliography. I prepared the figure legends and artists' statements and organized the biographical information on Storyteller artists presented in Part III, which records 379 Pueblo potters, 240 of whom have made Storytellers or related figures. Guy photographed the pieces which were to illustrate the book and did a good portion of the documentation on them as well. His color plates are in Part II of the book, while his black and white photographs are interspersed with the text in Part I. Parts I, II, and III all follow the same order of presentation: Pueblos are organized by language group, in order of relative importance to the development of the Storyteller figure — i.e., the Keres Pueblos first, followed by the Towa Pueblo of Jemez, the Tewa Pueblos, the Tiwa Pueblos, and Zuni Pueblo. Barbara and I shared interviewing and research on the artists, and all three of us constantly scouted for new artists at shows, museums, and galleries. Information on the artists was gathered primarily through personal interviews and mailed questionnaires.

As always in a book of this type, selection of illustrations was an extremely difficult task. Much as we regretted leaving out any, we were aware of the danger of repetition when dealing with a single theme. Our first concern was to present a fair representation for each Pueblo. In some, only one artist was working on the theme, but for large production centers — such as Cochiti, Jemez, and Acoma — our task was more complicated. For these areas we used longevity and productivity in the field as our criteria: we selected the work of potters who were the earliest makers of Storytellers and related figures (and whose work, thus, had historic significance) and that of potters who were the most prolific and consistent producers. We then viewed all of the works selected again from the standpoint of individuality of expression in order to provide as great a variety of interpretations as possible.

No doubt many more potters will have entered the field by the time this volume is published. Throughout the progress of the book we were constantly updating our lists, adding many new artists. Yvonne Lange, former director of the Museum of International Folk Art, made a comment on *Nacimientos* which is pertinent here: "It is rare that a movement is documented while it is occurring." As we can testify, it is rare because the book remains "in progress," as the authors attempt to include the newest artist or the most recent discovery. Although it was impossible to include all the artists active in the mid-1980s in this book, we are pleased to have been able to observe and document, both visually and in words, the history and early development of this new tradition in Pueblo figurative ceramics.

DORIS MONTHAN

Acknowledgments

 So many people have contributed to this book during the years of its making that it is impossible to thank them all individually. Many Pueblo potters welcomed us to their homes and gave us information — beyond their own biographical data — that made our task infinitely easier. Countless private collectors and gallery and museum people were gracious and invaluable in enabling our research. Among these, we owe a special debt of gratitude to the following individuals and institutions:

First and foremost, our thanks to Helen Cordero, who has shared her life and her art with us and without whom there would be no Storytellers. Our thanks, too, to Alexander Girard and Sallie Wagner, who encouraged Cochiti figurative potters and greatly assisted our efforts to document the pieces these artists created.

We are particularly grateful to Alexander E. Anthony, Jr., whose Adobe Gallery in Albuquerque became our first checkpoint on many trips to New Mexico. For many years he has focused on figurative art and has done much to stimulate awareness of it as a unique art form among collectors and to encourage Pueblo potters to enter the field. In Albuquerque we also had continuous access to Katherine H. Rust's fine Pueblo figurative pottery collection and to the generous hospitality of Bill and Barbara Douglas and David and Susie Jones.

Although each of us did not always have personal contact with some of these individuals, we are all equally grateful for the contributions they have made to this book. In Santa Fe and environs, there are several people to whom we are deeply indebted: Douglas Schwartz,

Director of the School of American Research, for a Weatherhead Fellowship (awarded to Barbara Babcock) that made initial research in New Mexico possible; Arthur Wolf, Director of the Millicent Rogers Museum, who took the time in 1978 to dig up old Cochiti figures long-buried in the basement of the Museum of New Mexico; Barbara Stanislawski, whose extensive knowledge and able assistance could always be counted on; Charlene Cerny, Associate Director of the Museum of International Folk Art, who put all the resources of the museum at our disposal from the beginning of the project; Letta Wofford, Rick Dillingham, Marjorie Lambert, Bob and Marianne Kapoun, Ray and Judy Dewey, Ruth Weber, Richard Spivey, and Forrest Fenn, all of whom shared their knowledge and collections of Pueblo pottery with us; Susan McGreevy, who has supported our research and who, as Director of the Wheelwright Museum, organized the first museum exhibit devoted to the Pueblo figurative tradition; Nancy Fox, Senior Curator of the Laboratory of Anthropology, who made it possible for us to document and photograph early Cochiti pieces; and Sandra and Bill Bobb of Cristof's Gallery, who generously allowed us to photograph figures from other Santa Fe dealers — The Kiva Indian Trading Post, Packard's Indian Trading Company, and Fenn Galleries, Ltd. — in their gallery studio. Others in Santa Fe made our task possible and pleasurable as well, by providing us creature comforts and intellectual stimulation: Chuck and Betty Lange, Dave and Aurea Warren, and, above all, Marsie and Peter Cate, Jacqueline Nelson, and Gene Meany Hodge, who gave us homes away from home. At Zuni Pueblo we are greatly indebted to Lorencita Mahkee and Margaret Hardin, who facilitated and assisted our research.

In our home state of Arizona we had invaluable assistance from many quarters. We are especially grateful to Dennis and Janis Lyon of Paradise Valley, who, like Alexander Girard, encouraged and assisted both Helen and us; to Michael and Susan Weber, who shared their Cochiti friends and collections; and to Larry Evers and Nancy Parezo of the University of Arizona, who shared our interests in Native American art and provided support and encouragement. Both the Wenner-Gren Foundation for Anthropological Research and the University of Arizona Humanities Committee awarded grants (to Barbara Babcock) that made it possible to conduct museum and ethnographic research and to obtain photographic documentation, for which we also wish to thank Glenn Short and Bradley Babcock. Birgit Hans was an invaluable library researcher and bibliographic assistant, and Jill Weber painstakingly typed and retyped the text and the bibliography. In Flagstaff, Dorothy Vaughter and Jody Ferrell, at the Museum of Northern Arizona

Gift Shop, and Dorothy House, Museum Librarian, helped in many ways. Last, but certainly not least, we want to thank Richard Diebold, who made our joint work sessions in Tucson far more productive and pleasant, lifting our morale and attending to our needs, always with the greatest tact and graciousness.

BARBARA A. BABCOCK
GUY AND DORIS MONTHAN

PART I

The Storyteller Tradition in Pueblo Culture

The Figurative Tradition

 One of the qualities of genius is the ability to experience mentally what has not been experienced sensually, and to embody this unique experience in tangible form. When such a person functions in the field of art, [s]he may produce those sudden mutations in style that mark the history of arts among all people. – Ruth Bunzel. *The Pueblo Potter.*

In April 1981, the Third Annual Storyteller Show opened at the Adobe Gallery in Albuquerque, and, in contrast to the gallery's first show in 1979, in which the work of ten Rio Grande Pueblo potters was represented, there were over two hundred figures by sixty-three potters. When I reported this substantial development in the Storyteller revolution to Cochiti potter Helen Cordero, she replied, "See, I just don't know. I guess I really started something."[1] And so, indeed, she did. When Helen Cordero shaped the first Storyteller doll in 1964, she made one of the oldest forms of Native American self-portraiture her own, reinvented a longstanding but moribund Cochiti tradition of figurative pottery, and engendered a revolution in Pueblo ceramics comparable to the revivals begun by Nampeyo, the Hopi-Tewa potter of Hano, and Maria Martinez of the Tewa Pueblo of San Ildefonso.[2] In the last two decades, Pueblo figurative pottery has been rediscovered, redefined, and reinvented by both producers and consumers. The "little people" that Helen Cordero has created have become prize-winning and world-famous collectors' items, and by the mid-1980s Storytellers and related figures were being made by more than 175 potters throughout the New Mexico Pueblos. In addition, figurines

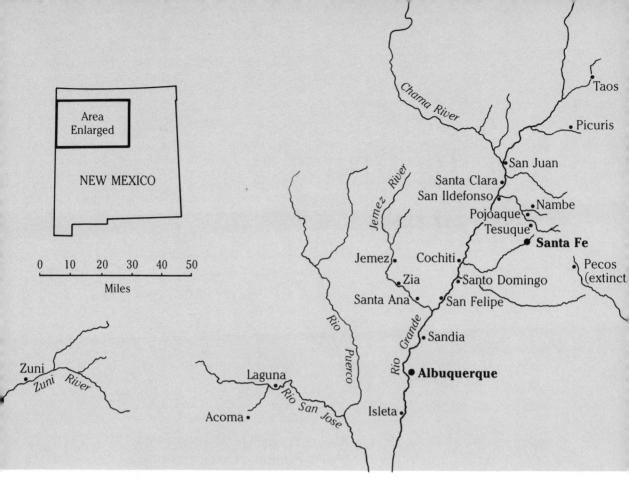

Map of the New Mexico Pueblos.

were being judged in categories other than "Pottery, Miscellaneous" and were regularly winning prizes at the Santa Fe Indian Market, sponsored by the Southwestern Association on Indian Affairs (SWAIA), and other major arts and crafts fairs throughout the Southwest; and galleries throughout the United States were having shows devoted entirely to figurative pottery. In the late 1970s and early 1980s, Sotheby Parke Bernet auctioned off old Cochiti figures for four-digit figures; and, for the first time in several centuries, Pueblo ceramic figurines began to be valued and respected as art.

Pueblo culture, which has endured in the southwestern United States for almost two thousand years, is distinguished both by its instinct for survival and its capacity to revitalize itself.[3] Without pottery to store water and grain, settled Puebloan existence as it developed in the first centuries A.D. and was lived until the last decades of the nineteenth century would have been literally inconceivable.[4] In the twentieth century, pottery has rarely been used for the storage, preparation, and consumption of foodstuffs, but it has become increasingly important symbolically and economically as a form of Pueblo cultural identity and survival.[5] The invention of the Storyteller and the attendant revival and expansion of figurative pottery making epitomize this capacity for revitalization, and the pages which follow document and describe these important changes and significant developments in the shape of Pueblo pottery.

Archaeologists conjecture that ceramic technology was introduced into what is now the American Southwest from Mesoamerica about 500 B.C. Within centuries, pottery making had become an integral element of the three major prehistoric sedentary cultures: the Hohokam of the southern Arizona desert; the Mogollon of mountainous eastern Arizona and southwestern New Mexico; and the Anasazi in the high plateau country of northern Arizona and New Mexico and southern Utah and Colorado.[6] In addition to utility ware, these Puebloan predecessors shaped and painted ceramic images of themselves, their gods, and the animals around them. The representative impulse in prehistoric pottery takes several forms: fetish, figurine, and effigy or effigy vessel, as well as both three-dimensional, appliquéd figures and two-dimensional, painted figures on nonfigurative and figurative shapes.

The term *fetish* can refer to any object used for a religious or ceremonial purpose. In Pueblo studies, however, it is used primarily to designate small zoomorphic figures carved from stone or wood or modeled from clay. Generally, the term implies the former method of manufacture, and unpainted clay creatures — even when used ceremonially — tend to be called figurines rather than fetishes.[7] *Figurine* or *effigy* usually refers to a free-standing, three-dimensional animal or human figure, which may be hollow or solid, depending on size. For the most part, *figurine* is used in conjunction with anthropomorphic forms. *Effigy*, of course, connotes religious use and has been widely used in preference to fetish or figurine for human figures carved from stone. The term *effigy vessel* — and sometimes just *effigy* — is used to describe a pottery vessel (such as a bowl, jar, or pitcher) wholly or partially shaped to form a three-dimensional representation of a human, animal, bird, or plant; in Hammack's terms, an effigy is "a non-functional embellishment of an artifact used primarily as a container."[8] Frequently, this embellishment involves nothing more, for example, than the shaping of a spout or a ladle handle into human or animal form. In addition, both two- and three-dimensional figures were used for decorative purposes on bowls, jars, and mugs as well as on figurines and effigy vessels. Two-dimensional anthropomorphic and zoomorphic figures in the form of painted figurative designs have also been found in all prehistoric Puebloan cultures, their finest and most abundant expression on the bowls made by the Mimbres branch of Mogollon culture between 750 A.D. and 1150 A.D.[9]

Both fired and unfired ceramic figurines of animals, birds, and humans have been found throughout the prehistoric Southwest, widely distributed in space and time.[10] Morss has argued that "the earliest known occurrence of figurines . . . in the whole Southwest is in the early pit house village of the Hilltop Phase known as Bluff Ruin, in Forestdale Valley in eastern Arizona, which is rather closely dated by a good cluster of tree-ring dates falling between A.D. 287 and 312."[11] Haury, however, dates Hohokam figurines found at Snaketown from the earliest, or Vahki, phase of the Pioneer Period, 300 B.C.–100 A.D. While the baseline for the figurine complex in the Southwest is debatable, there is no question that among the Anasazi true figurines were an integral element of Basketmaker III culture (400 A.D.–650 A.D.) and that the most common forms were human females. Most of these figurines consist of a minimally modeled slab or cylinder of clay no longer than six inches, with frontal orientation and perforated or appliquéd features; rarely are they painted or fired. The most interesting and elaborately modeled of Anasazi Basketmaker figurines are the Pillings figurines from northeast Utah (Figure 1) described by Morss.

In contrast to the great abundance and variety of painted figurative designs, especially Mimbres, there are seemingly few true figurines from the Mogollon. Such, however, is not the case for the Hohokam, at whose settlements the largest number of prehistoric figurines have been unearthed — at Snaketown in south-central Arizona, five hundred figurines were recovered from the first excavation alone. Hohokam figurines are similar to those of the Anasazi in size, shape, and subject matter — there is again a preponderance of human females with a frontal orientation. In contrast to Anasazi figurines, however, these are fired, exist in much greater numbers, and are found in a developmental sequence dating from about 300 B.C. to 1200 A.D.[12]

Like figurines, human and animal effigy vessels have been found in all three prehistoric southwestern cultures. The largest numbers of such forms are Anasazi in origin and date from Pueblo II and III (900 A.D.–1300 A.D.). In addition to effigy-handled vessels — such as mugs, pitchers, and jars, as well as ladles with "babe-in-cradle" handles — the most common effigy vessels are bird forms.[13] Inevitably, analyses of representational prehistoric art in general and of effigy vessels in particular lead archaeologists to look south, not only to the figurine complexes of the high cultures of Mesoamerica, but to Casas Grandes, the great trading center in what became northern Chihuahua. The largest community in the Southwest, Casas Grandes developed in the eleventh and twelfth centuries; between 1060 A.D. and 1340 A.D., it produced the finest of painted prehistoric effigy jars. The work of eleventh-century Casas ceramists was widely traded; Casas pottery (and its influence) has been found as far north as the great Anasazi Pueblo of Mesa Verde. Most of these polychrome figurative vessels are

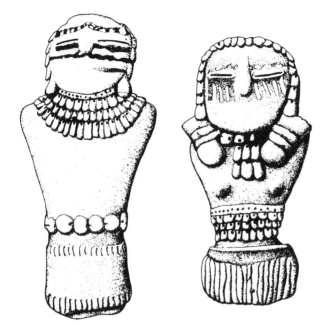

Figure 1. Pillings Figurines (northeastern Utah), 400 A.D. – 650 A.D.

Left: Unfired male figurine of cream-colored clay with basket impression on the back. He is much bedecked with red and buff facial paint, modeled hair, earrings, a multiple-strand necklace, and an elaborate belt, and is wearing a kilt incised to look like fringed leather. After Morss (1954: Figure 2). *Right*: Unfired female figurine of brown clay with basket impression on the back. She has incised eyes with black paint in the slits and red and buff facial paint above and below the eyes. Her hair, necklace, and belt are modeled, and the belt is accented with punctations; her apron is appliquéd and incised. After Morss (1954: Figure 7). Drawings courtesy of Clara Lee Tanner, *Prehistoric Southwestern Craft Arts* (Tucson: University of Arizona Press, 1976), p. 185, Figure 6.12.

Peabody Museum of American Archaeology and Ethnology, Cambridge, Massachusetts. Left: *6 inches high.* Right: *5⅜ inches high.*

human, and in both their modeled form and painted decoration bear a striking resemblance to historic Pueblo figurines and effigies, especially those produced at Cochiti Pueblo in the last half of the nineteenth century.[14] It does not seem possible that almost a thousand years elapsed between effigies such as the Casas mother and child shown in Figure 2 and the "Madonna" or "Singing-Mother" figures produced at Cochiti in the late 1800s and early 1900s.

What these ancestors of contemporary Pueblo figurative pottery mean and what they may have been used for have been subject to much debate and conjecture among both archaeologists and anthropologists. Some are of the opinion that small figurines and pottery miniatures in general were but children's toys. A larger number of scholars are inclined to regard both figurines and effigy vessels as religious in significance and use. On the basis of contextual evidence and other objects associated with figurines, Haury has suggested that Hohokam figurines "served as household 'gods' or adjuncts to house-blessing and fertility rites . . ., a means of securing increase of the family, of crops."[15] Given both the preponderance of female, anthropomorphic figurines and the ethnographic evidence from historic Pueblo culture, Morss, Renaud, and others have similarly argued for

Figure 2. Casas Grandes Mother and Child Effigy Jar (northern Chihuahua), 1060 A.D. – 1340 A.D.

This "hooded" effigy jar of Ramos Polychrome has a buff slip and primarily black painted designs. The base of the vessel, the lower half of the legs, and the body of the child are painted red. Many of its painted designs — the stepped clouds on the mother's cheeks, the rain lines on her chin, the checkerboard breastplate with seed dots, the banding line with triangles at her hairline, and the lightning lines on her left leg — are identical not only to Anasazi black-on-white pottery of the same period, but also to Kiua Polychrome vessels made at Cochiti and Santo Domingo in the nineteenth century and after, and to human figurines and effigy vessels produced at Cochiti between 1875 and 1900.

Arizona State Museum, Neg. No. 64018, Tucson, Arizona, Acc. No. 03724, 8 inches high.

THE FIGURATIVE TRADITION

connecting the Anasazi figurine complex to agricultural fertility cults and rites of human increase.[16]

On the basis of scattered ethnographic reports and investigations from the late nineteenth and early twentieth centuries, several relevant generalizations may be made about the use and significance of ceramic figures in historic Pueblo culture. There is no description of any Pueblo ceremony — be it for curing, hunting, rain, or fertility — or of any kiva altar that does not include both clay vessels, containing water and sacred meal, and effigies or fetishes made of stone, wood, or clay. It has been suggested that these objects, like the ceremonies and dances with which they are associated, function to maintain an equilibrium among the natural, supernatural, and social order of things.[17] Both two— and three-dimensional figurative designs may be described as embodiments of and prayers to ancestors, gods, or spirits for rain, for crops, for success in hunting, and for human and animal procreation.[18] That they were still so regarded in the 1980s is suggested by the fact that at Santo Domingo, the most conservative of the Keresan Pueblos, both painted and modeled figures were prohibited in pottery made for sale.

In traditional Pueblo belief, clay was regarded as a living substance and, as Cushing and others have pointed out, a pot acquired a kind of personal and conscious existence as it was being made.[19] "In other words, a pottery vessel was not thought of simply as an inert manufactured object. Rather, it was active, endowed with a life of its own. As a receptacle for water and food, it held, and was in turn, a source of life."[20] In addition to many stories which tell how the people came to make pottery, every recorded Pueblo origin myth also describes the creation of life itself as occurring in part through the process of pottery making. This is notably so in Keresan emergence stories in which Iyatiku ("bringing to life") and her sister, Nautsiti ("more of everything in the basket"), are sent up into the light, to this earth, by Itc'tinaku (Thought Woman, Spider Woman) with baskets crammed full of seeds and clay images from which they create all forms of life. Several of these seeds and "little images" actually enable the two sisters to reach their goal: the pine tree that they climb up, the badger who makes the hole in the earth big enough for them to climb through, and the locust who smooths the hole by plastering.[21]

A further indication of the association of clay figures with the creation, maintenance, and reproduction of Pueblo life is the practice of collectively representing Keresan townspeople in male and female clay images kept by the *cacique* (the religious leader of the Pueblo). As Parsons observed at Santo Domingo, the *cacique* "takes care of his people by looking after 'his children' just as the Mother (Iyatiku) whom he represents looked after the images in her basket." Similarly, among the Hopi, "when the chief of Awatobi invited the Oraibi chief to destroy Awatobi, he displayed two clay figurines, representing one, the townsmen, the other the townswomen. 'Here I have brought you my people,' calmly he said."[22] And, as Parsons also recorded throughout the Pueblos, small figurines, frequently unbaked and unpainted and made of cornmeal or clay, are central to rites and prayers of increase, particularly those associated with the winter solstice and Christmas. Images of domestic animals are placed on kiva or church altars and thereafter buried in the corral, "so that there will be more of them."[23] Florence Hawley Ellis has observed similar practices at Zia and, in 1977, Acoma potter Juana Leno told Doris Monthan of taking small, unfired animal figures to the church and placing them in a basket with wheat on the altar with the Nativity scene. After four days, the animals are taken home and buried in the corral where "they melt back into the earth from which they came."[24] Similarly, a woman wanting children would make a clay "baby," take it to the altar, and then place it on a small cradleboard in a special place in her home; or, she might be given a clay or wooden baby in a miniature cradle by one of the kachinas which she would then care for and regard as "the heart of the child."[25] Such clay figures are taken to be "the seed from which the real objects will grow."[26] Like some archaeologists, some ethnographers have argued that small animal figures in particular and pottery miniatures in general are nothing more than children's toys. Even if they are "toys," such "idle playthings" as clay horses or wooden kachina dolls have been regarded by the adults who make and give them as educational, as embodiments of supernatural personages or animal spirits, and as expressive of a ceremonial system as complex and as powerful as any known.

If modern scholars debate the religious significance of Pueblo figurative pottery, the Spanish clergy who arrived in the sixteenth and seventeenth centuries did not. They found *"muchos idolos"* throughout the Rio Grande Pueblos and were zealous in destroying them and discouraging further manufacture. In addition to punishment and wholesale destruction, the missionaries' favorite tactic was to denounce native religion as the work of the devil and to decry the making and using of indigenous images as witchcraft.[27] One consequence was the patterns of secrecy that developed, especially in the Rio Grande Pueblos, in the 1600s and have persisted to the 1980s. Another result of this persecution was the creation of a gap in the ceramic record of almost four hundred years between prehistoric figures and those collected and described in the last quarter of the nineteenth century. With the exception of some early Hopi Sikyatki Polychrome effigy vessels, a few polychrome effigy vessels and some small unfired animal figurines (1475 A.D.–1680 A.D.) from Hawikuh (the Zuni village that was destroyed in the Pueblo Revolt of 1680), and the simple figurines that Kidder excavated at the abandoned Pecos Pueblo and dated as Glaze V (1650 A.D.–1750 A.D.), there is no evidence of Pueblo figurative ceramics between circa 1500 and 1875.[28]

Despite the efforts of Spanish and then Anglo missionaries to stamp out Pueblo religion and "idolatry," the ceremonial system survived, together with its figurative painting, carving, and pottery traditions. When the railroads began to bring tourists to the Southwest after 1880, Rio Grande Pueblo potters sold them "odd and attractive pieces" as well as "utility pieces" (see Figure 3). In the late nineteenth century, almost all the Rio Grande Pueblos, in addition to Hopi and Zuni, made some human or animal figurative forms.[29] One example, a Zuni owl effigy, is shown in Figure 4. Anglos bought and sold these "grotesques" and "eccentrics," but they did not regard them highly, and the interest of traders, such as Jake Gold of Santa Fe, in promoting these ceramic "curiosities" became an excuse for disinterest on the part of serious students and collectors of Pueblo pottery who were inclined to dismiss historic figurines as commercial in origin, as "tourist art" at best (Figure 5).

As early as 1889, William Holmes published a note in the *American Anthropologist*, entitled "The Debasement of Pueblo Art," in which he urged not only that the manufacture of such forms be discouraged but that museums not deign to collect or accept them.[30] A few years later in his "Statement to the Trade for 1907," Thomas S. Dozier made the following remarks regarding pottery figures:

> No attempt will be made to describe these as it would necessarily lead to a discussion of the ceremonies themselves. . . . There is no doubt that children have been amused with pottery shaped to represent the human form, wholly or in part, or to represent the forms of the lower animals; perhaps, the makers themselves have learned to make new or strange forms from idle dallying in lazy moments; and it may be that many pieces considered ceremonial are but the results of these idle moments, or they may have been made simply to amuse. To this trait of character, not uncommon to more enlightened races, may be ascribed the reason for much of the pottery being made up and sold to the tourists, since the Indians derive some revenue from the sale of odd and attractive pieces, as well as from the utility pieces. . . . Education and a consequent learning of new duties will yet make an end of her pottery days . . . in this utilitarian age, she cannot always go on making toys.[31]

A PUEBLO GIRL SELLING CLAY IMAGES.
(From a Sketch by General Wallace.)

Figure 3. "Pueblo Girl Selling Clay Images," Lew Wallace, c. 1880s

This drawing, made by General Lew Wallace sometime after he was appointed
Territorial Governor of New Mexico in 1878, captures a roadside scene familiar to
visitors to New Mexico in the 1880s, and is the earliest documentation of figurines
made for sale to tourists. While Governor Wallace was administering the affairs of the
Territory and completing *Ben Hur* (1880) in the Palace at Santa Fe, his wife Susan "was
recording her interesting and lively impressions of the contemporary scene in letters to
an eastern newspaper, later published [in 1888] in a small book called *The Land of the
Pueblos*," with this sketch as the frontispiece (WPA Writers' Program 1940:132).

Frontispiece, The Land of the Pueblos *(1891 edition).*

Figure 4. Owl Effigy With Baby Owls (Zuni), pre-1879

This mother owl with her babies was one of many bird, animal, and human effigies collected by James Stevenson in 1879; he noted that all were twelve inches or smaller and painted white with brown and black decorations. This particular creature, which appeared as Figure 469 in the *Second Annual Report of the Bureau of American Ethnology* (1883), is one of several composite figures collected by Stevenson and is remarkably similar to those made in the 1980s not only at Zuni, but at Acoma and Cochiti, as well. Photograph courtesy of the National Anthropological Archives, Smithsonian Institution, Neg. No. 55014.

National Museum of Natural History, Washington, D.C., Acc. No. 40767, ca. 12 inches high.

Fortunately, "she" did go on making "toys." Unfortunately, something of this attitude remained with both scholars and collectors. As recently as the 1930s, when Kenneth Chapman and colleagues at the Museum of New Mexico were encouraging significant pottery revivals, they were discouraging the manufacture of figurative pottery. In her popular pocket handbook, *New Mexico Indians*, published in 1948, Bertha Dutton was also openly disparaging:

Figure 5. "Indian Pottery," by Ben Wittick, 1878–1881

This photograph of Cochiti and Tesuque figurines for sale at Jake Gold's Free Museum and Curiosity Shop was taken by Ben Wittick in a Santa Fe studio between 1878 and 1881. A very similar Wittick photograph was translated into an engraving that Gold used on his stationery and advertisements. The small seated figures in the foreground are the antecedents of the Tesuque Rain Gods which Gold later popularized and which, as evidenced by a 1904 invoice, were sold in bulk to curio dealers throughout the United States at $6.50 for one hundred Rain Gods. Cochiti potters produced the larger standing figures, many of which subsequently ended up in the attics and sub-basements of eastern museums.

Museum of New Mexico, Santa Fe, Neg. No. 16293.

At Tesuque, for instance, . . . most of the present output consists of the cheap, gaudily painted (with show card colors), novelty items [i.e., the popular Rain Gods] that are made expressly for the tourist trade. They cannot even be classed as true Indian ceramics, inasmuch as the decoration is applied after the pottery is fired. Jemez, Isleta, Cochiti, and Santo Domingo, lamentably, are also producing similar atrocities. However, in defense of the Indians, it should be explained that the idea for this type of product seems to have originated with a white man [very probably she is referring to Jake Gold].[32]

In their own way, the scholars were as successful as the padres, for rarely does one find historic figurines and effigy vessels in exhibits or books concerning Pueblo ceramic art, and until the late 1970s, there was not even a category for figurative forms at the Santa Fe Indian Market except "Pottery, Miscellaneous." This condescending attitude was evident as well in the Spanish word, *mono* (monkey, silly fool, mimic, mere doll), which was widely used by dealers and collectors until the late 1960s to refer to all figurines. Regrettably, George Swinton's remarks about attitudes toward Eskimo figurative sculpture apply with equal force to the treatment of Pueblo figurative ceramics:

> The inherently puritanical notions of the "functional hypothesis" on primitive art have prejudiced many social scientists and art historians against nonfunctional forms . . . in a very strange and totally unscientific way, we have developed a highly paternalistic ethnological purism and through it an unjustifiable anti-humanistic bias against these forms, against their artistic validity, and against the integrity of their producers.[33]

In addition to making Pueblo figurative ceramics more or less invisible, hidden away in countless museum basements and attics, the antifigurine bias contributed to a noticeable decline in the quantity and quality of figurative pottery throughout the Pueblos and resulted in a dearth of information about the many "curiosities" that have been collected since the 1870s.

For reasons we may never discover, the most sizeable, various, and continuous production of figurative shapes and designs has occurred in Cochiti Pueblo. The earliest historic Cochiti figures were collected by Col. James Stevenson of the Smithsonian Institution and by Rev. Sheldon Jackson, a Presbyterian missionary, in the late 1870s and early 1880s before the tourist boom. The majority of these figures are cream, terra-cotta, and black polychrome figurines and effigy vessels in human, animal, and bird forms which are frequently painted with figurative designs as well and which range from four to twenty-four inches in height. The iconography of these figures — clouds, lightning, and rain; seedpods, flowers, and corn plants; pregnant animals and hunting scenes — expresses again and again "the idea of fertilization" that Haeberlin described as the key symbol or root metaphor of Pueblo culture.[34] In female effigies — such as the small mother holding a child and dressed with corn plant designs (Color Plate 1), which Jackson collected and which is the earliest known Cochiti "Singing Mother" — the connection between human reproduction and other, life-giving forms of generation is explicitly made. It

Figure 6. Singing Mother (Cochiti), pre-1930

This polychrome woman carrying a rather large child on her back is representative of many "singing ladies" produced at Cochiti during the early twentieth century. In modeled and painted details, she resembles both earlier and later human figures made at Cochiti. The shape of her head and ears and her "coffee-bean" eyes are remarkably similar to figures made by Felipa Trujillo in the 1960s and 1970s.

Laboratory of Anthropology, Acc. No. 47939/12, Museum of New Mexico, Santa Fe, 6 inches high.

would seem that forms such as these — if not themselves used ceremonially — were, at the very least, reproductions of ceremonial shapes and designs.

What is certain is that as the presence of an Anglo market increased, the production of these types of figures declined. Museum data suggest that, except for occasional bird pitchers, effigy vessels ceased to be produced for sale after about 1880 and that, with few exceptions, animal and bird figurines became smaller and simpler. The shape of man, however, was dramatically transformed into much larger, standing figures. The earliest of these were, like the effigy vessels, painted primarily with figurative designs — birds, plants, rain clouds, etc. In what was probably a transitional phase, there was an abundance of standing male figures dressed biculturally with both Cochiti pottery designs and whiteman's garb, such as vests, boots, and bow ties. While figures of this sort continued to be made until shortly after the turn of the century, by 1880, Cochiti potters were producing an even larger and more distinctive human form whose painted garb was almost entirely Anglo and whose stance as well as attire had an unmistakable note of caricature and mockery. Between 1878 and 1881, when Ben Wittick took the photograph of "Indian Pottery" for sale in Jake Gold's Santa Fe shop (see Figure 5), and for at least another decade, Cochiti potters produced a profusion of Anglo professionals — cowboys, priests, businessmen, and carnival and circus entertainers, such as two-headed strongmen, dancing bears, and Italian opera singers. Whether the whiteman realized it or not, what he purchased and described as "primitive idols" or "eccentric grotesques" were, in fact, portraits of himself. The impetus for these humorous imitations was two-fold: along with tourists and assorted Anglo professionals, the railroad brought carnival, circus, and vaudeville to New Mexico; in turn, it took Cochiti men to Washington and New York where, among other things, they were introduced to the opera. Their mimings of countless versions of the whiteman in stereotypical operatic poses were re-presented in clay, as were the two-headed, no-legged freaks and dancing bears of the carnival and circus.[35] It is probably not coincidental that *mono*, the term used for these figures, was also used for figures that were knocked over or broken in carnival ball games. And it is not without interest that two Cochiti figurative ceramists, Louis Naranjo and Ivan Lewis, began re-producing caricature figures in the early 1980s. Naranjo has created a unique and humorous array of tourists with cameras, shorts, and bikinis, as well as priests and cowboys, while Lewis has become quite expert at imitating nineteenth-century figures such as Wittick photographed.

In the years between 1900 and 1960, there was a marked decline in both the quality and quantity of figurative ceramics produced by Cochiti potters. The human forms that were made were considerably smaller and more frequently portraits of themselves, rather than the whiteman — a drummer, a corn dancer, a woman with a child or a bowl of bread. And, with the exception of a few large birds and animals made by Estephanita Herrera, these forms, too, were much smaller and

Figure 7. Singing Mother (Cochiti), 1945–1955

This small, sparsely dressed mother with two children was probably never fired. The terra-cotta and black paints are the light orange and yellowish brown of clay paint and *guaco* before firing. Like many later Singing Mothers, she holds a child in each arm, wears her hair in a chongo, and has a squash blossom necklace. Not visible from this view is a back apron with delicate plant designs, an obvious antecedent of those worn by Ada Suina's female Storytellers.

Barbara Babcock Collection, Tucson, Arizona, 4 inches high.

Figure 8. Singing Ladies (Cochiti), 1955–1960

Left to right: Damacia Cordero, Teresita Romero, and Laurencita Herrera. These polychrome female figures made by three of Cochiti's well-known figurative potters exemplify the type of figures produced at Cochiti in the decade preceding the invention of the Storyteller. They hold, respectively, a baby in a cradleboard, a bowl of bread, and a typical Cochiti water jar (*olla*) with a pendant raincloud design. Drawing by Trudy Griffin-Pierce.

Left: *Laboratory of Anthropology, Museum of New Mexico, Santa Fe, Acc. No. 45967/12, 5½ inches high.*
Center: *Laboratory of Anthropology, Museum of New Mexico, Santa Fe, Acc. No. 25114/129, 7¼ inches high.*
Right: *Ruth Weber Collection, Santa Fe, New Mexico, 6 inches high.*

simpler than their turn-of-the-century prototypes. The consequences of the tourist demand for Indian-made souvenirs that could be easily carried back to Chicago are reflected as well in the pottery of other Pueblos. In addition to miniature bowls and jars and a number of non-Indian forms, such as ashtrays and candlesticks, Pueblo potters made an abundance of small human and animal figures for the tourists. While very few of these ever reached museum shelves, we do know that Zuni produced many smaller and less finely made owls; by 1920, Santa Clara potters were producing *animalitos* — small, polished, blackware birds and animals; and between 1900 and 1940, innumerable Tesuque Rain Gods were produced, initially at Jake Gold's instigation, and sold across the country in boxes of Gunther Candy.

When Edith Warner came to New Mexico in the 1920s, she purchased a mother and child figure from Cochiti, and "the girl who sold it to her called it the 'singing lady'."[36] The figure of a woman holding or carrying a child or two (Figures 6 and 7), which Cochiti potters called a "Singing Mother" or "Madonna," was the most popular human form made at Cochiti between 1920 and 1960. But only a few women, such as Teresita Romero, Damacia Cordero, and Laurencita Herrera, made them (Figure 8), and, as Helen Cordero has said, "for a long time pottery was silent in the Pueblo." In the mid-1980s, when pottery was anything but silent at Cochiti and over fifty potters were making Storytellers and related figurines, many potters would tell you that their mother or aunt or grandmother "made Storytellers a long time ago." They were referring, I have discovered, not to the Storyteller as later conceived and made popular by Helen Cordero, but to this Cochiti tradition of pottery mothers singing to their children.

The Invention of the Storyteller

 When Helen Cordero began making clay persons in the late 1950s, she was forty-five years old, the six children she had raised were grown, and she was doing beadwork and leatherwork with her husband's cousin, Juanita Arquero, to make a little extra money. Most of the profits, however, went for buying more materials, and one day Fred Cordero's aunt, Grandma Juana, said, "Why don't you girls go back to potteries? You don't have to buy anything; Mother Earth gives it all to you." And so, Juanita, who had learned to make pottery as a child, "started up again" and Helen spent six months "under her" learning the ancient art. Juanita was already an accomplished potter and, in comparison, Helen's bowls and jars "never looked right. They just kept coming out all crooked and I was ready to quit. I didn't think I would ever get it right." Juanita suggested that Helen "try figures instead," and "it was like a flower blooming" — small frogs, birds, animals, and, eventually, "little people" came to life in abundance.

One of the first times Helen "showed them out" at a Santo Domingo feast day, folk art collector Alexander Girard bought all the "little people" (standing male and female figures, eight to nine inches high) that she had; he also asked her to make more and larger figures and bring them to him, and shortly thereafter he commissioned a 250-piece Nativity set. Thinking, perhaps, of the "Singing Mothers" made by Helen (Color Plate 2) and several other Cochiti potters, Girard then asked her to make an even larger seated figure with children. Helen recalls that when she went home and thought about it, "I kept seeing my grandfather [Santiago Quintana]. That one, he was a really good storyteller and there were always lots of us grandchildrens around him."

In addition to telling stories to his many grandchildren and being known in the Pueblo as a gifted storyteller, a leading member of one of the clown societies, and a *"mucho sabio,"* Santiago Quintana (Figure 9) was a valued friend and collaborator to several generations of anthropologists and observers of Pueblo life. He wanted his traditions preserved and maintained and he went to great lengths to assure that

Figure 9. Santiago Quintana, ca. 1906

This photograph of Helen Cordero's grandfather, with one of his many grandchildren, was taken at Cochiti Pueblo. Courtesy of the Smithsonian Institution.

National Anthropological Archives, Washington, D.C., Neg. No. 80-5499.

they "got it right." Adolph Bandelier quoted from him at length in his journals and made him one of the protagonists in his ethnographic novel, *The Delight Makers* (1890), situated in Frijoles Canyon, to which he was first taken by Santiago; in 1897, Frederick Starr recorded most of his Cochiti census from Santiago, also traveled with him to Frijoles Canyon, and greatly enjoyed his company; in *Indians of the Terraced Houses* (1912), Charles F. Saunders recounted a conversation with Santiago about his trip to California; Edward S. Curtis photographed him and quoted him extensively in Volume 16 of *The North American Indian* (1926); and Ruth Benedict collected many Cochiti tales from him and wrote warmly of him in letters from the field. In the Introduction to *Tales of the Cochiti Indians* (1931) she described him as follows:

> Informant 4 was a very different individual from the others, as can be seen in the material recorded from him. He spoke Spanish fairly, and had been an adventurer all his life. He is very old now, but a leading member of the *principales*, in great demand in those acculturated Mexican ceremonies in which repartee must be carried on in what is considered to be Spanish. He liked best to give true stories . . . and his tales of the mythological heroes always emphasized their success in turning the mockery that had been directed against them against those who had mocked them.[37]

When Helen remembered her grandfather's voice and shaped that first image of him telling stories to five grandchildren in 1964, she made two significant modifications in the Singing Mother tradition: (1) she made the primary figure male, rather than female, and (2) she placed more than a realistic number of children on him. This first Storyteller (Color Plate 3) had five children; subsequent ones have had as many as thirty.

Almost immediately the Storyteller brought Helen Cordero acclaim and success. In 1964, her figures were awarded first, second, and third prizes at the New Mexico State Fair, and in 1965, a Storyteller won a first prize at SWAIA's Santa Fe Indian Market. As her work improved with each passing year (see Color Plate 4), both her reputation and the demand for her work continued to grow: there have been more "ribbons" than she can count, both at Indian Market and at the Heard Museum's Annual Indian Arts and Crafts Show; pottery-making demonstrations from Pecos National Monument to Kent State University; inclusion in national and international exhibits, notably the First World Crafts Exhibit, "In Praise of Hands," in Toronto in 1974; and shows of her own at Indian art shops and galleries throughout the country, beginning with The Hand and the Spirit Gallery in Scottsdale, Arizona, in 1973. In addition to being included in numerous southwestern museum shows, Helen has been honored with two museum exhibits of her own — at the Heard Museum in 1976 and "Tales for All Seasons," a major retrospective exhibit at the Wheelwright Museum in 1981–1982. And, in October 1982, she received one of the ninth annual New Mexico Governor's Awards for Excellence and Achievement in the Arts. A month later, one of her Storytellers (Color Plate 5) appeared on the cover of *National Geographic* in conjunction with a feature essay on Pueblo pottery. Ten years earlier, in April 1972, *Sunset Magazine* had also featured a Helen Cordero Storyteller on its cover together with an article on Southwest Indian art. It was after this that the demand for her work increased markedly and her reputation began to extend far beyond the southwestern United States. Like it or not, Helen's "little people" made her a famous Pueblo potter ("a big Indian artist"), bringing people from all over the world to her home in Cochiti Pueblo and more orders for Storytellers than she could possibly fill. When asked about her success, she has said, "I don't like to be called 'famous.' My name is Helen Cordero. It's my grandfather, he's giving me these."

In addition to considerable professional and material rewards, this widespread recognition of and demand for Storytellers has had several important consequences. In Helen's own work, it resulted in both technical refinements and the invention of new forms. As a result of increased sanding and applications of white slip before painting, the finish of Helen's figures became finer. In the late 1960s, she began making the children separately and appliquéing them, rather than pulling them out of the primary piece of clay. This technique enabled her not only to increase the number of children, but to vary their placements and postures, and it made for much greater success in firing. "When I did it the old way, the little kids would pop off in the fire and I lost a lot of pieces." By the early 1970s her Storytellers not only had more children and finer painted garb, but the main figure itself had become taller, thinner, and better proportioned (see Color Plates 4 and 5). "Those first ones were fat and I couldn't get his face right." By 1970, she had also developed the distinctive face which has become her trademark: "His eyes are closed because he's thinking; his mouth is open because he's singing" (see Color Plates 4 and 5). About the same time, she began signing her pieces by printing her name and Cochiti Pueblo on the bottom in *guaco*. Most of the Storytellers that Helen produced in the 1960s were either unsigned or signed in script in pencil or pen after firing.

Helen's success with Storytellers and the demand for her work also led her to produce other images of her experience, other family and cultural self-portraits. In addition to Nativities,[38] Singing Mothers, and Storytellers, she created during the 1970s and 1980s a Drummer, a Pueblo Father, a Nightcrier, a Water Carrier, a Hopi Maiden, an Owl, a Turtle, a Praying Storyteller, a Navajo Storyteller, and a Children's Hour. Many of Helen Cordero's "potteries"[39] bear the imprint of her husband, Fred Cordero. When she first started, Helen was afraid to paint her people, and Fred both taught her and helped her to paint for several years. Later, he assisted by making miniature drumsticks for the Drummers and cradleboards, bows and arrows, and stables for her Nativities. Her Drummer is a portrait of Fred who, in addition to being a fine drum maker, has been the leading singer and drummer for the Pumpkin Kiva and has held many ceremonial and political offices in the Pueblo, including Governor. Like the Drummer, the Nightcrier — the only large, standing figure that Helen makes — is also a familiar Cochiti ceremonial figure, and sometimes he, too, is personalized by being given a Governor's cane of office "so that he looks like Grandpa" [Fred]. Helen made the first Nightcrier in 1976 after she saw an old (1880–1900) standing Cochiti figure at Fenn Galleries in Santa Fe. She looked at it standing in its *nicho* on the stairway and said, "He's sad. Nobody should sing alone." So, she measured it and went home and made the first of these large, standing figures, who now sings with his century-old friend.[40]

One interesting variation on her original Storyteller is the Praying Storyteller that Helen first made in the mid-1970s, in which the story-teller is in a kneeling rather than a seated position, with the children scrambling over his legs behind him. In those days, when countless customers were vying for Storytellers, one Phoenix collector got down on his knees and begged Helen for a Storyteller, threatening to stay in that position until she made him one. Helen laughed in recalling, "Right after that I made him one, and he got his Storyteller all right — on his knees." In the spring of 1984, Helen began to experiment with what she called her Navajo Storyteller: instead of having legs, the base of this figure extends out into an apron on which the children are placed, completely encircling the figure. (For a similar variation by other potters, see Figure 38 and Color Plate 27). Another representation of the storytelling theme is the Children's Hour, first made in the early 1970s, in which the children are separate pieces grouped around, rather than attached to the storyteller. In describing this figure (Color Plate 6), Helen said, "These are older kids listening to him. My grandpa used to say, 'Come children, it's time,' and I remember us all around him out at the ranch in the summer, and that's how I thought of the Children's Hour."

Despite these variations and the other figures in her repertoire, the Storyteller has remained her favorite and the most requested. Although she has made hundreds (Figure 10), no two are identical — not only do the children vary enormously in their number, placement, postures, and painted detail, but the Storyteller himself has several hairstyles (braids, knotted in a chongo, long and free-flowing, or cut short),

Figure 10. Helen Cordero at Work, 1979

In this photograph, taken in the dining room of her Cochiti home, Helen Cordero was shaping a Storyteller with twenty-five children for an exhibit at the Denver Museum of Natural History.

Denver Museum of Natural History, Denver, Colorado, Neg. No. 4-79082-9A.

appears with or without hats and headbands, and has a great assortment of shirts (plain white, terra-cotta, or black ones, plaids, stripes, flowered calico, Jemez-style embroidered ones, and ribbon shirts, such as Pueblo men wear on feast days). And, sometimes, the shirts are treated as pottery rather than cloth and painted with traditional Cochiti pottery designs. After trying in vain to estimate how many Storytellers she had produced since 1964, I asked Helen how many "little people" she had made during the past year or just in the last month. She replied, "I really don't know. It's like breads, we don't count."

The Revival of Pueblo Figurative Ceramics

 If it is impossible to determine how many Storytellers Helen Cordero has shaped since 1964, it is even more difficult to assess the influence of her invention, which began a remarkable revival of figurative pottery both in her own and other New Mexico Pueblos. By 1973, when the Museum of International Folk Art in Santa Fe mounted its "What Is Folk Art?" exhibit, Storytellers were being made by at least six other Cochiti potters — Felipa Trujillo, Aurelia Suina, Juanita Arquero, Frances Suina, Seferina Ortiz, and Damacia Cordero. Most of these artists continued to make figures and became well-known and awarded for their creations (Figure 11). In the mid-1980s, no less than fifty-five Cochiti potters, including several members of Helen's own family, were making figurines.

Keres Pueblos

Cochiti. During the late 1970s and early 1980s, Helen's son, George Cordero; her daughter, Tony; her grandchildren, Tim Cordero (who lives in Tuba City and works at Cochiti with Helen in the summer), Kevin Peshlakai, and Buffy Cordero; her son-in-law, Del Trancosa from San Felipe, and her foster daughters-in-law, Kathy Trujillo (originally from San Ildefonso) and Mary Trujillo (originally from San Juan) all "started on Storytellers." Examples of the work of some of these relatives are shown in Figures 12–15 and Color Plate 7.

Kathy Trujillo learned to make pottery as a child from her parents,

Jose A. and Rosalie Aguilar, and, until she moved to Cochiti and began making polychrome figures, she made black-on-black ware. During the 1970s and 1980s, Kathy's brothers, Alfred Aguilar and Jose V. Aguilar, Sr., were among the best and most famous of San Ildefonso's figurative potters. Her sisters, Florence Naranjo and Annie Martinez, also were potters, and in 1977, her daughter, Evon Trujillo, began making figures. The development of Mary Trujillo's work has been especially remarkable. In the early 1980s, she became one of the best Cochiti potters, producing not only Storytellers, but also Nativity and Corn-Husking Scenes and Storyteller Turtles and Lizards (Figure 15 and Color Plate 7) and winning prizes and doing shows and demonstrations. Mary learned to make pottery from her mother, Leonidas Tapia, a fine San Juan potter, and, after moving to Cochiti in 1978, benefited from the advice and assistance of both Helen Cordero and her neighbor, Ada Suina, another master figurative potter.

Ada Suina made her first Storyteller in 1976 and has won prizes for her Storytellers, Drummers, or Nativities almost every year since she first entered Indian Market in 1976.[41] Her figures (Figure 16 and Color Plate 8) are distinguished by their extremely fine workmanship, their

Figure 11. Cochiti Storytellers in the "What is Folk Art?" Exhibit, 1973

At an exhibit sponsored by the Museum of International Folk Art in Santa Fe, seven Cochiti artists were represented: (*left to right*) Helen Cordero, Felipa Trujillo, Aurelia Suina, Juanita Arquero, Frances Suina, Seferina Ortiz, and Damacia Cordero. The figure in the center is one of the very few Storytellers produced by Helen's teacher, Juanita Arquero, whose artistry is primarily expressed in the finest of contemporary Cochiti bowls and jars.

Museum of New Mexico, Santa Fe, Neg. No. 70433.

Figure 12. Tim Cordero (Cochiti), Male Storyteller, 1980

Son of the late Jimmy Cordero and his Hopi wife Lenora Holmes, Tim started making pottery between 1979 and 1980 while living in Cochiti with his grandmother, Helen Cordero. This figure is one of the first pieces he made, at age sixteen or seventeen. Major areas of the figure are a light beige, with terra-cotta and black painted accents. As in Helen's figures, the adult's eyes are closed and the mouth is open. The mustache and outstretched arms, however, are Tim's distinctive variations.

Barbara Babcock Collection, Tucson, Arizona, 1 child, 6 inches high.

Figure 13. Del Trancosa (Cochiti), Male Storyteller, 1980

Born in San Felipe, Del Trancosa later lived in Cochiti and learned to make Storytellers from his mother-in-law, Helen Cordero. This figure, made in 1980, was among his first. It is well modeled and finely detailed, and resembles Helen's adult males, particularly her Pueblo Father. Like Helen's "The Children's Hour" (see Color Plate 6), this Story- teller holds a cigarette (here made of rolled corn husk), representing the practice of ceremonial smoking that accompanies the telling of sacred stories.

Fenn Galleries, Ltd., Santa Fe, New Mexico, 1 child, 8½ inches high.

Figure 14. Three Cochiti Storytellers, 1981

Left to right: Mary Trujillo, Male Storyteller; Kathy Trujillo, Male Storyteller; Mary Frances Herrera, Miniature Female Storyteller. These figures illustrate the many variations in size, shape, and detail in Storytellers from the same Pueblo. All three figures are modeled in Cochiti clay, with the typical black and terra-cotta detailing.

Left: *Private Collection, Flagstaff, Arizona, 4 children, 8 ½ inches high.*
Center: *Adobe Gallery, Albuquerque, New Mexico, 1 child, 5½ inches high.*
Right: *Adobe Gallery, Albuquerque, New Mexico, 6 children, 1½ inches high.*

"In San Ildefonso Pueblo, where I was born, I made the traditional black-on-black pottery, but when I moved to Cochiti, I began working with figures. Then Dorothy Trujillo encouraged me to make Storytellers and helped me. Now I work with Mary Martin, and she has helped me, too."

Kathy Trujillo
Cochiti

Figure 15. Mary Trujillo (Cochiti), Lizard Storyteller, 1981

Both the adult lizard and baby lizard bear saddle-shaped designs on their backs — the baby's is checkered and the mother's has the scallop border of traditional Cochiti vessels. The lizard figure is frequently appliquéd on Cochiti water jars and other pottery forms, but it is not often seen as a separate figure. This piece, like most Cochiti animal figures, is gray with black detailing.

The Kiva Indian Trading Post, Santa Fe, New Mexico, 1 baby, 2½ inches high.

> *"Everything I use is the traditional Cochiti material — Cochiti white clay for my figures, the white slip, and bee plant for the black paint."*
>
> **Mary Trujillo**
> **Cochiti**

large and very distinctive faces, and the addition of an unusual pale orange or apricot to the traditional polychrome. Ada did not make pottery herself until 1975 and learned to do so from her mother-in-law, Aurelia Suina, and her cousin, Virginia Naranjo, both of whom have made Storytellers and animal figures. In addition to helping Mary Trujillo, Ada has shared her skill with four of her daughters, who have made Storytellers as well as Nativities and animal figures. In 1978, Ada's sister, Stephanie Rhoades, also began making Storytellers — one of her figures took third prize at the 1982 New Mexico State Fair (Figure 17), and in 1983 both Stephanie and Ada's daughter, Marie Suina, won prizes at Indian Market.

Three of the Cochiti potters featured in the 1973 Folk Art exhibit in Santa Fe — Seferina Ortiz, Aurelia Suina, and Frances Suina — have Storytellers on permanent display in the Indian Pueblo Cultural Center in Albuquerque. Aurelia and Frances Suina learned to make figures as well as traditional vessels in the 1920s. In the 1940s and 1950s, both these potters made small Singing Mothers with children which they later referred to as "Storytellers." After Storytellers became popular in the late 1960s and early 1970s, both began making larger, seated figures with many children (Figures 18 and 19) in addition to Nativities[42] and animal figures. A distinguishing feature of Frances Suina's large, male Storytellers is the use of traditional Cochiti vessel designs — rainclouds, lightning, and rain, scallops and stepped terraces with negative leaf motifs — on the back of the Storyteller's shirt.

Frances has passed on her skill and her style to her son and daughter-in-law, Louis and Virginia Naranjo, who have become well-known and awarded for their Nativities and Storyteller animals, as well as Storytellers and caricature figures. One of Virginia's first prize-winning figures was a small turtle. She continued to make these creatures, many of them storyteller-style, like the one shown in Figure 20, with small turtles riding on the shell of the larger one. After Storytellers became popular, many Cochiti, Santa Clara, and Jemez potters turned from *animalitos* to larger animals with babies, which they also called Storytellers. Virginia's husband, Louis, was the first potter to make Bear Storytellers, which range in size from three to fifteen inches and come in a variety of shapes. Many, like the one featured in Color Plate 9, assume the classic Storyteller posture — a large, seated bear holding baby bears on its lap and in its arms; others are on all fours with the babies on their backs. The mother or father bears are always black and the babies terra-cotta.

Seferina Ortiz was born into a long line of figurative potters. From the first decades of the twentieth century until 1960, her great aunt, Estephanita Herrera, known in the Pueblo as "Grandma Honey," continued the nineteenth-century tradition of very large animal and bird figurines and bird effigy pitchers. Seferina learned to make pottery in the 1960s from her mother, Laurencita Herrera (see Figure 8), one of the few potters making human figurines in the decades before the Storyteller. She, in turn, taught three daughters and a son to make figures. In the 1970s and 1980s Seferina not only won prizes for her Storytellers (see Figure 11) and Drummers, but also became especially adept at Storyteller animals, such as Lizards, Turtles, and the Frog and Owl Storytellers shown in Figures 21 and 22. Her figures frequently include traditional Cochiti pottery designs as well as naturalistic

Figure 16. Ada Suina (Cochiti), Female Storyteller, 1980

The long, floral patterned mantilla is one feature that sets this female Storyteller apart. Other features, which have become Ada Suina's trademarks, are the large head, the modeled, realistic nose, the open mouth (with the suggestion of teeth), and the pale orange color added to the traditional black, cream, and terra-cotta. In this figure, the pale orange is alternated with terra-cotta in the flowers on the mantilla and is used for the blouse and hem border of the manta.

Adobe Gallery, Albuquerque, New Mexico, 2 children, 8½ inches high.

Figure 17. Stephanie Rhoades "Snow Flake Flower" (Cochiti), "Sounds," 1982

Pieces by Stephanie Rhoades, the sister of Ada Suina, are signed with the potter's Indian name, "Snow Flake Flower." She started making pottery part-time in the late 1970s, and the male Storyteller shown here took third prize at the 1982 New Mexico State Fair. This piece makes use of the lightning symbol, and, to further illustrate the rain theme, the adult is holding a gourd rattle, which is used in Pueblo rain ceremonies. Another repeated motif is the bear paw-print.

Adobe Gallery, Albuquerque, New Mexico, 2 children, 8½ inches high.

Figure 18. Aurelia Suina (Cochiti), Female Storyteller, 1981

Some identifying features of Aurelia Suina's Storytellers are the open, widely spaced eyes, set high on the forehead; the small, modeled nose; and a tiny, horizontal, open mouth. Pieces by this artist are noted for their fine patina, achieved by careful preliminary sanding and then polishing of the slip. The female Storyteller illustrated here wears a blouse with a suggestion of embroidery on the sleeves, the traditional manta, and boots. The cradle with a baby in it, resting on her legs, is removable. For an earlier example of her work, see Figure 11.

Adobe Gallery, Albuquerque, New Mexico, 4 children, 6½ inches high.

Figure 19. Frances Suina (Cochiti), Male Storyteller, 1981

This noted artist began making pottery around 1927. Her son, Louis Naranjo, has recalled that as early as 1945 she was making figures with babies. Here, her male Storyteller holds a boy and girl, who resemble miniature adults. Patterning on this figure is well defined: the little girl holds a decorated bowl, and the back of the Storyteller's jacket has a rain-cloud motif. Predominant colors are grayish beige with black and terra-cotta detailing. One of her female Storytellers appears in Figure 11.

Adobe Gallery, Albuquerque, New Mexico, 2 children, 6½ inches high.

painted details, and her owls are very similar both to those made at
Zuni for over a century and to those made on a large scale by Estephanita Herrera and on a much smaller one by Teresita Romero at
Cochiti in the 1950s. Since 1975, Mary Priscilla Romero, Teresita's
daughter-in-law and pupil, has also produced an abundance of small
Storyteller Frogs and taught her daughter, Mary Eunice Ware, to make
figures as well.

Until her mother, Estephanita Herrera, died in 1960, Felipa Trujillo
assisted her in making large bowls, effigy pitchers, and figurines. After
that she began making figures "on her own." Her husband, Paul Trujillo
(who was Helen Cordero's maternal uncle), helped Felipa by gathering
the clay and doing the sanding until he died in 1983. In addition to
Storytellers (Color Plate 10; see also Figure 11) and Singing Mothers,
Felipa has made a wide variety of prize-winning figures, including
several favorite Cochiti forms: the "Pottery Maker" (a large seated

Figure 20. Virginia Naranjo (Cochiti), Turtle Storyteller, 1981

Virginia Naranjo, noted (along with her husband, Louis) for animal figures, received
an award for one of her composite turtles in 1973; since that time both she and her
husband have won many major prizes. This Turtle Storyteller is fashioned from native
clay and, like most Cochiti animal figures, is predominantly gray with black detailing.
The artist has added a touch of bright terra-cotta to the mother turtle's mouth, and has
used a variety of traditional Cochiti design motifs: vertical stripes on the mother's head,
double scallops on her shell, and a hatched checkerboard on the shells of the babies.

The Kiva Indian Trading Post, Santa Fe, New Mexico, 3 babies, 3 ½ inches high.

Figure 21. Seferina Ortiz (Cochiti), Frog Storyteller, 1981

This versatile artist began making "all kinds of small dolls and animals" in the early 1960s. The frog is a traditional subject among Cochiti potters, and here it is depicted with two baby frogs on its back and a small bird or fly in its mouth. The predominant color is light gray, with black detailing; traditional water motifs (a rain cloud and a fish) are painted on its back. Seferina, also noted for her human Storytellers, Drummers, Nativity sets, and what she has called "Family Sets" (a man and wife with children), has won many prizes for her figures.

The Kiva Indian Trading Post, Santa Fe, New Mexico, 2 babies, 3¾ inches high.

> *"My mother, Laurencita Herrera, taught me how to make pottery in 1961, and the first Storyteller I made was about 1962. Mom was making the small figures, so she told me to try, and I did. My great-aunt, Estephanita Herrera, made Storytellers in 1952. Then it died out and Helen began."*
>
> **Seferina Ortiz**
> **Cochiti**

Figure 22. Seferina Ortiz (Cochiti), Owl Storyteller, 1983

The large owl holding four baby owls in its wings was fashioned in native Cochiti clay and is predominantly gray with black and terra-cotta detailing. Seferina's work often has unexpected touches, such as the fir-bough pattern on the large owl's wings. She has said, "I do all my Storytellers by coiling and shaping them. I don't use any special tools or techniques — I just make as I go along and see what comes out." One of her human Storytellers is shown in Figure 11.

Museum of Northern Arizona Gift Shop, Flagstaff, Arizona, 4 babies, 8½ inches high.

woman holding a pot), Frogs (similar to those made by her kinswoman, Seferina Ortiz), and Drummers. Like Fred Cordero and many other Cochiti men, her husband also made prize-winning drums. In 1969 she began making Nativities[43] distinguished by a baby Jesus in a ceramic cradleboard, similar to the "babes-in-cradles" that Pueblo potters have made for centuries.

Another well-known Cochiti potter, Damacia Cordero, had been making human and animal figures for over fifty years when she turned to Storytellers in the 1970s and 1980s. Two of her earlier works are illustrated in Figures 8 and 11; Figure 23 shows a Storyteller made in 1980. Not surprisingly, her figures have a much older look about them and, as a consequence of her firing technique, are much grayer in color than most Cochiti figures. Damacia taught all four of her daughters to make pottery, "but only two, Martha Arquero and Josephine Arquero, are constantly making it," and they, too, have made human and animal figures. Martha has won prizes at both Indian Market and the New Mexico State Fair for her Frog and human Storytellers. One of her most appealing creations, and certainly the most unusual of animal Storytellers, is a kangaroo with a baby in its pouch and pottery designs on both pouch and chest (Figure 24).

After Dorothy Loretto married Onofre Trujillo and moved to Cochiti in the 1950s, Onofre's aunt, Damacia Cordero, taught her to use Cochiti clays and assisted her in making figures. In the mid-1970s, she began to win prizes for her Storytellers and her Nativities[44] at Indian Arts fairs throughout the Southwest, and has participated in shows and demonstrations in several states. Both the style[45] and colors of her figures (Color Plate 11) differ somewhat from those associated with Cochiti, and with good reason. Dorothy was born in Jemez and learned to make pottery as a child both from her mother, Carrie Reid Loretto, a native of Laguna, and her Jemez grandmother, Lupe Madalena Loretto. She is the oldest of the six Loretto sisters, all of whom have made Storytellers and among whose work there is a distinct family resemblance as there is in the work of Dorothy's three daughters and her son Onofre II, whom she has taught to make Storytellers and related figures. Dorothy also taught her friend, Mary Martin, to make Storytellers. Since 1975, when she made her first one, Mary has made a variety of distinctive Storytellers, Drummers, and Singing Mothers, as well as Nativities.

In 1979, the "One Space, Three Visions" exhibit that opened the Albuquerque Museum included the work of seven Cochiti figurative potters. In addition to the work of Helen Cordero, Laurencita Herrera, Seferina Ortiz, Teresita Romero, Ada Suina, and Aurelia Suina, the exhibit contained a small and distinctive Storyteller made in 1977 by Rita Lewis. Rita began making Storytellers about 1973 with her Acoma

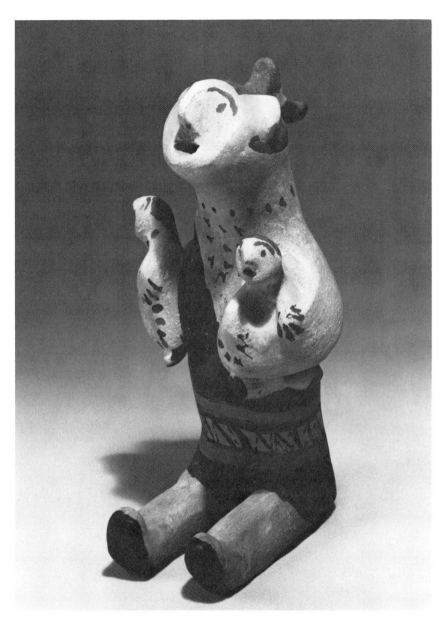

Figure 23. Damacia Cordero (Cochiti), Female Storyteller, 1980

Damacia began making pottery around 1920 and was making Singing Mother figures in the 1950s (see Figure 8). Her Storytellers, which are quite distinctive, give the impression of having evolved from a much older figurative tradition. They are easily recognized by their straight, elongated torsos; long, arched noses that extend from the hairline; and protruding ears, exaggerated to the point of resembling fins or wings. Modeling of the adult's arms and of the two babies' bodies is minimal, and that characteristic, too, sets her figures apart. The female Storyteller shown here has just the suggestion of a patterned blouse, while her manta and sash are clearly defined. One of Damacia's somewhat more complex Storytellers is shown in Figure 11.

*Alexander E. Anthony, Jr., Collection, Albuquerque, New Mexico, 2 children,
8½ inches high.*

Figure 24. Martha Arquero (Cochiti), Kangaroo Storyteller, 1982

Though the kangaroo is an unusual subject for a Cochiti potter, Martha Arquero has adapted it comfortably to traditional Cochiti styles and materials. This kangaroo, carrying a baby in its pouch, is embellished with pottery designs and, like other Cochiti animals, is gray, with black and terra-cotta detailing. Martha has also made deer and elephants, as well as the more traditional frogs, turtles, and human Storytellers.

Adobe Gallery, Albuquerque, New Mexico, 1 baby, 7 inches high.

"I use the clay we get from the nearby hills; same way with the red paint. The black I make myself from wild plants. I fire my pieces outside with cowchips and plenty of wood."

Martha Arquero
Cochiti

husband, Ivan, and since 1980 they have consistently won prizes at Indian Market. One of their unique figures is shown in Figure 25. The son of Lucy Lewis, and member of a large family of prize-winning potters, Ivan distinguished himself in the early 1980s with his reproductions of nineteenth-century Cochiti caricature figures. After seeing old Cochiti figures, as well as photographs of them, displayed in the Wheelwright Museum show in 1981–1982, Ivan decided to try them, and, with Rita's assistance in copying the old pottery designs, he successfully revived these forgotten forms. In the early 1980s, both their daughter Patricia and their daughter-in-law Mary also began making figures.

Another male potter, Tony Dallas, from the Hopi village of Moencopi, also introduced a new form into the Cochiti Storyteller repertoire in the early 1980s. With the assistance of his mother-in-law, Lucy R. Suina, he began making pottery in August 1982, and by December of that year he had tried his hand at a Storyteller. What came out was a predominantly terra-cotta mudhead clown, holding a bowl and covered with tiny replicas of itself (Figure 26). Mudhead clowns are a common and unforgettable sight at Hopi dances, and Tony's figures, with "a lot of action in them," resemble both their ceremonial prototypes and mudhead kachina dolls. Because Cochiti potters are enjoined against making and selling clown and kachina figures, only Tony Dallas and Tim Cordero, both from Hopi, were producing clowns and Clown Storytellers in the 1980s.

Students of ethnic arts are inclined to regard miniaturization as an indication of the commercialization and popularization of a traditional art form.[46] Although Cochiti Storytellers were, from the beginning, made almost exclusively for sale to the Anglo market, they became obviously "commercialized" and even more popular after 1978 when Mary Frances Herrera made the first miniatures (see Figure 14). These Storytellers of less than two inches sold for thirty-five dollars and initiated a "little tradition" of very small and, for the most part, much less expensive Storytellers. Storytellers from three-quarters of an inch to three inches (in contrast to "normal" size of about six inches and up) were later made by several other Cochiti potters and many Jemez imitators. Commercialization is also evident in the use of acrylic paints after firing on the otherwise very fine and interesting Storytellers made by Margaret Quintana, Louise Q. Suina, and Vangie Suina. Even when the color range is restricted to black, white, and terra-cotta polychrome, as in Vangie's pieces (Figure 27), the colors are much more intense than those produced by traditional mineral and vegetal paints. Vangie's Storytellers have superb detailing and have won prizes at Indian Market in the "Non-Traditional" category.

While every potter has her own special techniques and tools and some may use different clays to produce a distinctive color, almost all Cochiti potters have used traditional methods to create their Storytellers. Older potters, such as Helen and Damacia Cordero, have been quite adamant that old methods be followed, and Helen has even attributed her success to the fact that she makes her potteries "in the old way, the right way." The only concessions they have made to modern technology are to use camel's hair instead of yucca brushes, and sandpaper as well as or instead of polishing stones to smooth the figure, the considerable complexity of modeled detail in Storytellers with large numbers of children demanding the use of sandpaper. Clays for the figure, the white slip, and the red paint as well as pumice for temper are gathered on or near the reservation. The black paint, or *guaco*, is produced by boiling "wild spinach" (Rocky Mountain bee plant) into a sludge which hardens into a cake that is used like watercolor paint.

After pounding, sifting, mixing, and kneading the clay, most potters use two methods to shape their figures — very small figures and the children that are attached to the Storytellers are solid and begin as a cylinder of clay; the torso and head of larger figures and Storytellers are hollow and are usually built up in coils like a bowl or jar. The figures are allowed to dry for several weeks and are then sanded, slipped several times with a thin white clay, painted with *guaco* and terra-cotta, and fired. Firing is "the hardest part" and all potters have their "secrets," but most Storyteller makers use some sort of grate or support under which a cedar-wood fire is laid; the potteries are placed on top of this grate, protected with chicken wire or sheets of metal, and covered

"My husband and I both work together. For our Storytellers we use our Cochiti red clay and sometimes the white clay, and our natural paints — black made from the bee's plant, and the red. We coil them and they are hollow inside; for tools we have broken gourds and popsicle sticks. I fire them the old way, outdoors, with manure and cedar wood. My husband started making cowboys several years ago. We went to museums and saw figures, some with two heads. He made cowboys from then on, and I painted the old designs we copied. He keeps getting orders, and I know he enjoys making them."

Rita Lewis
Cochiti

Figure 25. Ivan and Rita Lewis (Cochiti), Female Storyteller, 1980

This husband-and-wife team started making bowls and animals together around 1971, and Storytellers in 1973. The female figure here has seven children (one is on her back) and a puppy. The distinctive hands of the five children on the sides are not modeled, but flow into the figure of the woman. Patterning on the clothes is intricate and well defined, and the hair style is a departure from the usual chongo knot. The Lewis team's figures won six major awards at Indian Market between 1979 and 1983.

Adobe Gallery, Albuquerque, New Mexico, 7 children, 9¼ inches high.

with a dome of cow or sheep dung. This "oven" produces a very intense oxidizing fire that is allowed to burn down before the coals are scattered and the potteries removed. To produce their blackware figures, Santa Clara potters smother the fire with pulverized manure, creating a reducing atmosphere that causes carbonization.[47] Some potters at Cochiti and other Pueblos have used a cut-off steel drum to create an outdoor oven that will guarantee no smudging or "fire-clouds," and others have resorted to firing inside in a gas or electric kiln.

When Alexander Anthony, owner of the Adobe Gallery in Albuquerque, organized his first Storyteller Show in May 1979, five Cochiti potters — Helen Cordero, Dorothy Trujillo, Mary Frances Herrera, Rita Lewis, and Seferina Ortiz — participated; in the gallery's fourth show in 1982, there were twenty-three potters. A similar increase was reflected in the number of Cochiti potters exhibiting at SWAIA's Indian Market: in 1979, nine potters sold Storytellers; in 1983, twenty-six did so. In the mid-1980s, not only were more Cochiti potters selling and winning prizes for their figures at Indian Market, but more prizes were being given. In 1971, a Helen Cordero Storyteller (see Color Plate 5) won a first prize in the "Traditional Pottery, Painted, Miscellaneous" category. By 1980, there were so many fine figurines that separate categories had been designated under each of the major pottery classifications for "Single Figures," "Storytellers," and "Sets and Scenes," in addition to "Miscellaneous." In that same year, Cochiti potters Ada Suina, Rita Lewis, Josephine Arquero, and Aurelia Suina all won prizes for Storytellers and other figurative forms, such as Drummers and Nativities. In 1983, ten Cochiti potters took away thirteen prizes, including four firsts, for figurines.

While these other Cochiti Storytellers share many features in common with Helen Cordero's, the differences are significant. With a few notable exceptions, most of them are smaller, less complex, and less technically proficient. More importantly, the majority are female figures with a marked frontal orientation. They are not grandfather figures and they are not, as far as Helen Cordero is concerned, "really" Storytellers. "They call them Storytellers, but they don't know what it means. They don't know it's after my grandfather." As frequently happens with the popularization of an art form, a design appeals and sells and is reproduced with little or no reference to or awareness of its origins or original meaning. But, if Helen's grandfather was unique, her experience was not, and one of the reasons that Storytellers became so popular is that other potters were able to relate them to their own experience of a favorite aunt or grandmother or grandfather who told them stories. Nonetheless, as Helen's remarks imply, one of the prob-

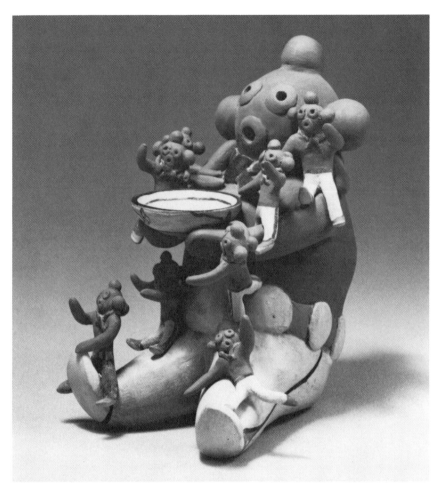

Figure 26. Tony Dallas (Cochiti), Mudhead Storyteller, 1982

Tony Dallas, a Hopi who moved to his wife's Pueblo, began making pottery under the tutelage of his mother-in-law, Lucy R. Suina, in the summer of 1982. His first pieces were bowls and pitchers with lizard appliqués, but after a few months he decided to try a Storyteller. The adult shown here wears a large concho belt and holds a platter, while eight little mudheads play on his arms and legs. Heads and upper torsos are terracotta, while the trousers and platter are light cream with a few black accents.

Adobe Gallery, Albuquerque, New Mexico, 8 children, 5½ inches high.

"I started to make a regular one [Storyteller], but then I thought, 'Mudheads tell stories, too,' so I began making them. . . . I try to put a lot of action in them."

Tony Dallas
Cochiti

Figure 27. Vangie Suina (Cochiti), Female Storyteller, 1981

In 1980, Vangie Suina left a business career to stay at home with her two young daughters. Five months later she began making Storytellers, with some instruction from her mother, Louise Q. Suina. Most of the children on this figure are holding something — pots, alphabet blocks, drums, balls of all types, an apple, a watermelon, and a baby (held by the large child in the center). The woman wears a back apron over a detailed costume and a necklace of najas. Vangie has created hundreds of variations since this early piece and has won numerous prizes.

Cristof's Gallery, Santa Fe, New Mexico, 22 children, 12 inches high.

lems in talking about Storytellers in Cochiti as well as other Pueblos is a certain amount of terminological confusion. By the mid-1980s, the word "Storyteller" was attached to much more than the figure conceived and invented by Helen Cordero in 1964. Not only have Singing Mothers made in the 1940s and 1950s been described as "Storytellers" (see, for example, Seferina Ortiz's statement with Figures 21 and 22), but the word has been used in conjunction with almost *any* composite human or animal figurine. In sum, "Storyteller" has become, as *mono* once was, a generic term for pottery figurines.

As the number and proficiency of figurative potters increased at Cochiti, so did the imitators in other New Mexico Pueblos. What is remarkable is not that other Pueblos began to produce clay figures in addition to bowls and jars, but the rapidity with which the production of figurines in general and Storytellers in particular has increased since the mid-1970s. In the fall of 1977, there were only about fifteen Storyteller potters, the majority of whom were from Cochiti. Within a year, that number had doubled and included notable additions of Acoma and Jemez potters. By the fall of 1979, it had doubled yet again to no less than sixty potters, with almost as many from Jemez as from Cochiti. That same year all of the eighteen potters exhibiting figures at the Eight Northern Pueblos Arts and Crafts Fair were from Pueblos other than Cochiti: Jemez (10), Acoma (4), Nambe (2), Isleta (1), and San Felipe (1).[48] Three of the Jemez potters — Marie Romero and her daughters, Laura Gachupin and Maxine Toya — won prizes for their figurines. Marie Romero and Maxine Toya won prizes again a month later at the 1979 Indian Market for figurative forms including Storytellers, as did one Isleta, four Acoma, and five Cochiti potters. While

"*As a little girl, I always wanted to sleep at my grandmother's house because I liked to hear her tell about the old times. My father-in-law, Eufrasio Suina, is an important man in our Pueblo and has many things to tell us. Often, when we go to their house, we will sit around the dining-room table and talk until one o'clock in the morning. He tells us how they used to do things, how to use knowledge gained from experience, things that happened in the past, how to get along better.*"

Vangie Suina
Cochiti

Cochiti potters took away most of the prizes that year (Ada Suina alone won three firsts for a Storyteller, a Drummer, and a Nativity), for the first time there were more potters from Jemez than from Cochiti selling Storytellers. In all, forty-one figurative potters exhibited at the 1979 Indian Market (thirty-two of whom were from nine Pueblos other than Cochiti): Jemez (11), Cochiti (9), Santa Clara (8), Acoma (6), Nambe (2), Tesuque (1), San Ildefonso (1), San Felipe (1), Taos (1), and Isleta (1). Between 1979 and the mid-1980s, the number of potters making Storytellers and related figures and winning prizes for them more than trebled: by August of 1984, there were over 190 figurative potters from fourteen of the nineteen New Mexico Pueblos.[49] With the exception of twenty men, these potters were women and, in addition to the fifty-five from Cochiti, they were distributed as follows: Jemez (63), Acoma (28), San Felipe (2), Santo Domingo (1), Zia (1), Taos (3), Isleta (5), Tesuque (4), Nambe (6), San Ildefonso (6), San Juan (1), Santa Clara (19), and Zuni (4). In some cases, the potter's Pueblo affiliation was by marriage,[50] but most were producing pottery in the Pueblo in which they were born and in the style associated with that Pueblo. The idea of the Storyteller and the polychrome Cochiti model has been translated into the various distinctive local clays, paints, and designs: an Acoma Storyteller is as unmistakable as an Acoma pot, and so it is with Jemez and Santa Clara.[51]

Acoma. Potters at Acoma, the western-most Keres Pueblo, were making bird figurines and effigy vessels for sale in the late 1800s. In the 1970s and 1980s, the Pueblo became famous for its very fine black-on-white pottery and for the revival of prehistoric Mogollon designs. Frances Torivio Pino started shaping figurines in the 1940s and was, very probably, the first Acoma potter to make Storytellers in the late 1960s. One of her Storytellers made in 1980 is shown in Color Plate 12. By the mid-1970s, two of her daughters, Lillian Salvador and Wanda Aragon, were also making Storytellers as well as Nativities and bird and animal figurines. Their Storytellers are distinctive in that the bottom half of the figure is painted with traditional Acoma pottery designs and is shaped like an effigy jar, with or without a bottom, to which legs may or may not be added. A 1984 owl Storyteller by Wanda Aragon (Figure 28), a 1978 Female Storyteller by Rose Torivio (Figure 29), and a 1983 Male Storyteller by Ethel Shields (Color Plate 13) all exemplify this style and are characteristically Acoma Polychrome, with its fine paste; thin, hard walls; stark-white, kaolin slip; and predominance of fine-line, black design. In the 1980s, as Marilyn Henderson has admitted, many

Acoma potters fired their work in kilns, making for an even chalkier white surface.

Ethel Shields began making Storytellers after she moved back to Acoma from Tucson in 1978, and, in addition to making figures that seem to emerge from a bowl or jar (such as Color Plate 13), she has made vessels to which she appliqués figures. One of her more appealing creations is a traditional stepped bowl filled with children

Figure 28. Wanda Aragon (Acoma), Owl Storyteller, 1984

Miniature owls were among the first things Wanda Aragon created when she started making pottery in the late 1960s, and she continued to experiment with them in figures such as this one. She has produced owls with bodies shaped like inverted pots which are decorated with typical Acoma pottery motifs in black-on-white, to which she often adds terra-cotta. In this example the owls are white with black detailing and have tiny touches of terra-cotta on their beaks and encircling the pupils of their eyes.

Guy and Doris Monthan Collection, Flagstaff, Arizona, 2 babies, 2¾ inches high.

Figure 29. Rose Torivio (Acoma), Female Storyteller, 1978

In this unique interpretation the woman's skirt is shaped like an inverted bowl with bold, geometric designs in black and terra-cotta; note the way the artist has altered the design in front to accommodate the extended legs. The rest of the adult figure and the two babies are defined with a minimum of detail. String tied in the loop of the chongo knot streams down the back.

Barbara Babcock Collection, Tucson, Arizona, 2 children, 5 inches high.

climbing out and over the side. Several of her children, notably her son Jack, have joined her in making Storytellers. Like other figurative potters, Ethel also makes Nativities.[52] The largest, most complex and innovative Acoma Storytellers have been produced by Marilyn Henderson, who also started in 1978 and won a second prize the first time she entered Indian Market in 1982. While her figures are not shaped or painted like bowls or jars, almost every Storyteller she has made holds a pottery vessel. The composition of a 1980 female Storyteller (Color Plate 14) is centered around an Acoma canteen; a 1983 male Storyteller (Figure 30) drinks from a canteen with a rainbird design, and one of the children drinks from a miniature canteen as well.

The combination of vessels with figurines, characteristic of Acoma Storytellers, reflects the fact that the majority of these potters were making bowls and jars long before they tried their hands at Storytellers. This was certainly the case with Juana Leno, one of Acoma's master potters who began as a child in the mid-1920s and first produced Nativities[53] and Storytellers in 1976. Since then she and her five daughters have made a variety of Storytellers and figurative forms in addition to traditional shapes. The same pattern obtained for Juana Pasqual and her daughters, Blanche Antonio and Mary Lukee, who have made both large and miniature bowls, jars, and wedding vases as well as figurines.

Most Acoma Storytellers date from the mid- to late 1970s and, while considerably smaller in size and quantity than the Cochiti prototype, they are of consistently high quality. Since 1975, Wanda Aragon and Hilda Antonio, Rose Torivio's sister, have regularly won prizes at Indian Market for their Storytellers and Storyteller Owls. Although she has not made Storytellers, Stella Shutiva has produced superb all-white corrugated ware and has won prizes in the 1970s and 1980s both for her large, corrugated bird and animal figures and for her vessels.

"We have to work hard to get the clay we use for our potteries. You can only drive vehicles so far; then we must walk at least three miles, much of it up a steep cliff, which can be dangerous. For our yellow paint we use quicksand, and getting that can be risky, too."

Rose Torivio
Acoma

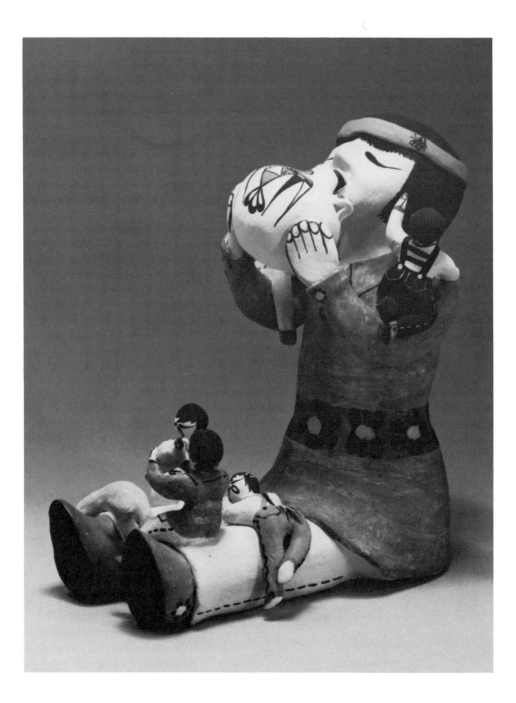

Figure 30. Marilyn Henderson (Acoma), Male Storyteller, 1983

This figure illustrates Marilyn Henderson's "new style" — a male Storyteller drinking from his canteen. One of the children sitting on his legs also drinks from a miniature canteen. Like her earlier versions, the pottery vessels show careful detailing (the adult's canteen bears a finely executed rainbird design), but here there is much less decoration on the adult's and children's clothing. The figure is modeled in native clay with a white slip and decorated with natural paints of black and terra-cotta.

Adobe Gallery, Albuquerque, New Mexico, 5 children, 9½ inches high.

Santo Domingo. In three other Keres Pueblos, only four potters have made Storytellers. None of them are native to the Pueblos where they have lived and worked since 1973, and none of them have produced pottery in a style characteristic of that Pueblo. Despite their proximity to Cochiti, Santo Domingo potters have been enjoined for over a century against making figures for sale. The one woman there who has made Storytellers, Marie Edna Coriz (another of the Loretto sisters from Jemez), was encouraged to do so in 1978 by her sister Dorothy Trujillo, who lived across the river in Cochiti. Stylistically, her Storytellers are very similar to those of her sisters — they have widespread legs, very abstract faces with small round mouths, Roman noses, crescent-moon eyes, and a distinctive buff-colored slip, which is darker than the cream color characteristic of Cochiti and lighter than the tan slip used by the majority of Jemez potters. Some of her figures — like those of her sisters Fannie Wall Loretto, Lupe Lucero, and Alma Concha Loretto — are entirely buff and terra-cotta; others, like the one shown in Figure 31, are buff, terra-cotta, and black polychrome, resembling the works of sisters Dorothy Trujillo and Mary E. Toya. Marie Edna Coriz has won prizes for her work both at Indian Market and at several California fairs.

San Felipe. Several miles down the Rio Grande at San Felipe, two women — one of them another Loretto sister, Leonora (Lupe) Lucero, and the other Dorothy Trujillo's daughter, Cecilia Valencia — have made Storytellers since the mid-1970s. Lupe's figures are made of Jemez clays and paints and are painted exclusively in buff and terra-cotta. In addition to her Storytellers (Color Plate 15), Lupe has produced Drummers, Nativities, and small Tourists with cameras and baseball caps. In the mid-1980s, she made a figure she called "The Pottery" (a woman holding a miniature pot), that is very similar to Marilyn Henderson's 1980 Storyteller (see Color Plate 14) and to Cochiti self-portraits made decades earlier. Lupe has never entered her work at markets and fairs, but her niece Cecilia has, and has won prizes at Eight Northern Pueblos, the New Mexico State Fair, and the Heard Museum Show.

Zia. Adrienne Shije, the only potter who has made Storytellers at Zia, was also born in Jemez. She made her first Storyteller in 1980 after watching Alma Concha, and subsequently was assisted by Marie Romero as well. The influence of both women is evident in her fine work — her light-colored, male Storytellers (like the one shown in Figure 32) resemble Alma's, while her female figures, with much more black and terra-cotta, are like Marie's. Finding the Zia clay "too sticky," she has used Jemez clays for her figures as well as the buff slip and red

Figure 31. Marie Edna Coriz (Santo Domingo), Male Storyteller, 1981

Born in Jemez, this potter moved to Santo Domingo when she married and began to use her adopted Pueblo's native clays and paints. The Storyteller shown here illustrates several features characteristic of this artist's work: widespread legs, crisply tailored trousers, looped arms with hands clasped over the chest, and the large, prominent nose. The hair is modeled in a chongo knot, with a loop through which yarn is tied (a technique her five Loretto sisters have also sometimes employed).

Adobe Gallery, Albuquerque, New Mexico, 4 children, 6½ inches high.

> *"Storytellers show that Indian people have a lot of character and would like to share their humanity and pride with all people. Stories are important to us because that is our way of life and, if it weren't for these stories, we would be very ignorant of our ancestors."*
>
> **Marie Edna Coriz**
> **Santo Domingo**

Figure 32. Adrienne Shije (Zia), Male Storyteller, 1981

Adrienne was raised in Jemez, but moved to Zia in 1975. Her Storytellers are modeled of Jemez clay and detailed with black mineral paint from Zia and red and white clay paints from Jemez. The major surfaces of this figure are light cream, with terra-cotta used sparingly for the adult's headband and for details on the clothing; black is reserved for hair and facial features.

Adobe Gallery, Albuquerque, New Mexico, 4 children, 5½ inches high.

> *"My little daughter, Erin, aged one, loves the babies on my Storytellers. She's always trying to take them off. I think she's jealous. Sometimes I spend more time with them than with her. I tell her, 'They're your little brothers. You can't be mean to them.'"*
>
> **Adrienne Shije**
> **Zia**

paint. The black details on her figures are Zia mineral paint. In the mid-1980s, Adrienne was still learning to fire and taking her pieces back to Jemez to be fired. She was also learning Zia pottery methods from her mother-in-law, master potter Eusebia Shije, and beginning to make small bowls with the distinctive Zia painted bird design.[54]

The Towa Pueblo of Jemez

When Odd Halseth, Kenneth Chapman's assistant at the School of American Research, visited Jemez in 1924, "no pure Jemez-made pottery had been produced in the past one hundred years. What pottery was produced at Jemez had been made by potters from other Pueblos who had married into that Pueblo."[55] He showed the potters photos and drawings of old Jemez designs which he encouraged them to use, and within a year Jemez pottery was exhibited at the 1925 Indian Fair in Santa Fe. Since the 1920s, there has been considerable experimentation at Jemez with various decorated styles, materials, and techniques, including kiln-fired commercial colors and glazes and painting after firing with poster paints and acrylics. By the mid-1960s, a style of geometric designs in strong tones of brown on a tan ground was fairly well established. This color pattern has been maintained through the mid-1980s in the majority of Jemez Storytellers and other figurines, which are distinguished by their tan slip and dark brown (as well as black and terra-cotta) painted designs.

Jemez has long been noted for its "tourist trinkets" and small figurines, and several of the older potters reported making Singing Mothers painted with poster paint in the 1950s, but it was only in 1968 that Marie Romero and her mother Persingula Gachupin made the first Storytellers. After the mid-1970s, there was a dramatic increase in Storyteller production, and by the mid-1980s, there were over sixty potters in Jemez, in addition to seven Jemez potters in other Pueblos, making figurines. This remarkable boom, as well as an accompanying return to traditional techniques and materials, is difficult to explain in a Pueblo not otherwise noted for pottery production. One obvious factor is economic. By the mid- to late 1970s there was an expanding market for figurines. Few could obtain or afford a Helen Cordero Storyteller for $1,500 or more, but well-made figures for $25 to $250 sold as fast as they were made, and Jemez potters capitalized on this market. Another factor was Marie Romero, who taught pottery making at the Jemez Day School during this time period and who assisted many other younger potters outside the classroom as well. One of Marie's pupils was Edwina (Bonnie) Fragua, who started in 1978 and by 1981 was winning prizes at the Eight Northern Pueblos fair and at Indian Market. Perhaps the most important factor contributing to the rapid expansion of Jemez figurative production was the presence of several very large, extended, pottery-making families: the daughter (Marie Romero) and granddaughters of Persingula Gachupin; the five Fragua sisters — the daughters of Grace Fragua and granddaughters of Emilia Loretto; their cousins, the six Loretto sisters — the daughters of Carrie Reid Loretto and nieces of Loretta Cajero — and their children as well — notably the seven daughters of Mary E. Toya. For more information on these and other Jemez potters and their interrelationships, see Part III.

Persingula Gachupin began making pottery in the mid-1920s and first shaped her Storytellers around 1968, after watching her daughter, Marie Romero. She continued to make them, in addition to other figurative forms, such as Nativities and Owls covered with baby owls. The Storyteller featured in Color Plate 16, made in 1980, uses what has become a common and distinctive feature of Jemez figures — the storyteller or storytelling scene is placed on and attached to a flat disc or plate of clay; this feature is also seen in Marie Romero's "Hunter Storyteller" (Figure 33), an interesting variation on what Helen Cordero called "The Children's Hour." Marie's classic Storytellers — for example, the one shown in Color Plate 17 — are also distinguished by an extension of the Storyteller's skirt into a footrest under the figure's legs. After making the first Storytellers at Jemez in the late 1960s, Marie went on to make other figures — including the first Nativity[56] in 1975 — and was one of the first Jemez potters to win prizes for her figures. Since 1976, she and her daughters, Maxine Toya (Figure 34) and Laura Gachupin, have consistently produced excellent figurative pottery and have been awarded for their work.

The six Loretto sisters and their children are another very productive, prize-winning, pottery family. In the mid-1980s, three of the sisters were living and working in other Pueblos (Dorothy Trujillo, Lupe Lucero, and Marie Edna Coriz), but Alma Concha Loretto, Fannie Wall Loretto, and Mary E. Toya were living and working in Jemez. Mary and Alma learned to make figures when they were children. Alma made her first Storytellers in 1969 after she moved to Taos, and Mary began about 1973. Fannie, who had studied art and ceramics at Fort Lewis College, learned to make traditional figures from her sisters in 1974 and made her first Storyteller in 1978. Alma's Storytellers are entirely buff and terra-cotta, a style that several of her sisters have imitated. Hers are distinguished by their terra-cotta faces with no painted features and by their Taos-style braids (Figure 35). Her mudhead figures, which usually reverse the color pattern of her Storytellers, are also well-known. Earlier figures were seated and held a pottery bowl or jar; later she

Figure 33. Marie Romero (Jemez), Hunter Storyteller, 1980

Marie Romero, the first potter in Jemez to make Storytellers (1968), became a major force in the development of fine figurative art in her Pueblo. The scene shown here is a variation in which the separate figures are attached to a clay disc (9½ inches x 7½ inches). The disc and major portions of the figures are buff, with black and terra-cotta for other areas. The hunter, with his dog beside him, tells of his adventures; each of the boys has his own wooden bow and arrow, and one of them has a canteen just like the hunter's, decorated with a corn-stalk design.

Adobe Gallery, Albuquerque, New Mexico, 3 children, 5¼ inches high.

> *"For making my Storytellers I use native Jemez clay and white sand. First I make the base; then I coil the body, and I make the arms, legs, and head separately. The finished figure is then dried; after that I sand it and paint it with earth paints made of red and black rocks. Finally, I fire it in the traditional way — outdoors, using old roofing tin to set it on and cedar wood for fuel."*
>
> **Marie G. Romero**
> **Jemez**

Figure 34. Maxine Toya (Jemez), Mother and Child, 1981

An age-old theme in Pueblo (and worldwide) art is beautifully interpreted here by one of the younger generation of potters. Maxine referred to it simply as a Mother and Child, rather than a Storyteller, Modeled in native Jemez clay, the figure has a light, buff-colored slip and painted details in black, terra-cotta, and brown; these four colors are a distinctive aspect of Maxine's work. She has created at least eight different figurative subjects and has won prizes for each of them.

Adobe Gallery, Albuquerque, New Mexico, 5½ inches high.

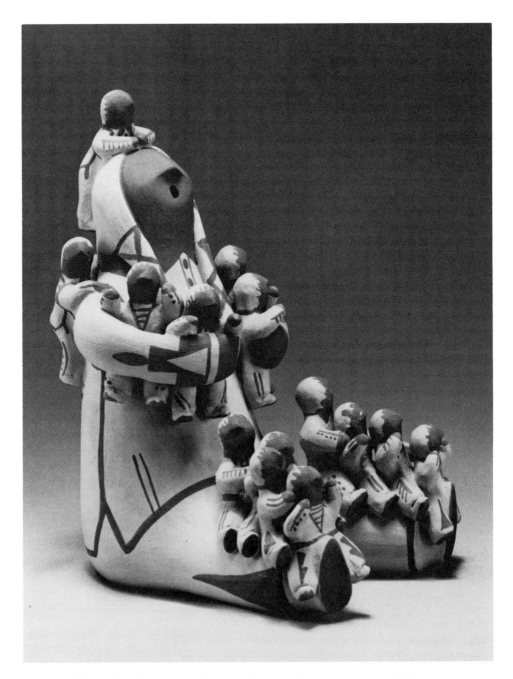

Figure 35. Alma Concha Loretto (Jemez), Male Storyteller, 1982

This Storyteller wears his hair in the braided Taos style, typical of the many figures Alma made during her residence in that Pueblo. A light, cream-colored slip is used for the major portions of the clothes and hair, and the faces are terra-cotta. Minimal detail on the faces is one of this potter's trademarks; here, the children have no facial features except modeled noses and the adult has only a modeled nose and modeled open mouth. The artist has won numerous prizes, and one of her Storytellers is in the collection of the Smithsonian.

Adobe Gallery, Albuquerque, New Mexico, 15 children, 9 inches high.

created Mudhead Storytellers, incorporating not only feathers, but black painted details (Color Plate 18). Like several of her sisters, Alma has made miniatures as well as full-size Storytellers and Nativities,[57] and she, too, has been a consistent prize-winner.

In addition to winning countless prizes, Mary E. Toya has produced not only the largest number of daughters making Storytellers (seven), but the world's largest Storyteller (Color Plate 19). This Storyteller, made in 1984, took six months to make and has 115 children. In 1982, Mary won a first prize at Eight Northern Pueblos for a Storyteller with fifty children, a record at that time. Inspired by that success, she went on to produce two Storytellers (in 1982 and 1984) with one hundred children each before making "the world's largest." In addition to Storytellers and Nativities, she has made and won prizes for large bowls and wedding vases, all buff, black, and terra-cotta polychrome. If she has made some of the largest, she has also made some of the smallest — miniatures only three-quarters of an inch high, all of them very finely painted.

Fannie Wall Loretto has also made some of the smallest and largest of Jemez Storytellers. Fannie's Storytellers are made exclusively in terra-cotta on buff, and are distinguished from those of her sisters by a cape on the adult figure on which is painted a sun kachina design. The Storyteller pictured in Figure 36, one of the largest she has made, won a third prize at Eight Northern Pueblos in 1982. In addition to the faces and the buff slip already discussed, another distinctive feature of the Loretto sisters' larger Storytellers is the large number of children held high in the Storyteller's arms, creating the impression of a necklace of children.

Like Persingula Gachupin, Loretta Cajero began making pottery in the mid-1920s. She decided to try Storytellers in the late 1970s after seeing what had happened with her nieces, the Loretto sisters. She, in turn, taught her daughter, Frances Casiquito, and her grandson Gabriel to make figures. Loretta's figures have a tan ground with dark brown designs associated with earlier Jemez pottery and are placed on a clay disc (Figure 37). Loretta is also the aunt of Carol Pecos, who has recalled that her grandmother (Loretta's mother), Lupe Madalena Loretto, made figures in the 1920s: "She really knew how to make people. I don't know where all that pottery has gone."

Carol Pecos learned to make pottery as a child from her mother (and Loretta's sister), Louisa Toledo, but didn't make Storytellers until about 1974, when she discovered "it was a lot of fun creating and getting better." Carol has experimented constantly and in the 1980s began making Storytellers on a clay base, both covered with and surrounded by children (Color Plate 20). In addition to traditional

Figure 36. Fannie Wall Loretto (Jemez), Male Storyteller, 1982

Originally, this artist did contemporary figures with a sculptural feel, but in the late 1970s, she returned to a more traditional Pueblo style. This large male Storyteller took third prize at the 1982 Eight Northern Pueblos Exhibit. Most of the children are arranged on the front of the adult figure, who has a painted sun design on the back of his cape. In the early 1980s, Fannie and some of her sisters began signing their pieces with the water symbol (two double U's) next to their names, since their mother was of the Water Clan.

Adobe Gallery, Albuquerque, New Mexico, 43 children, 14 inches high.

Figure 37. Loretta Cajero (Jemez), Female Storyteller, 1981

This artist began making pottery in the mid-1920s but first started doing Storytellers in the late 1970s. Individual features of this figure include the closed mouth and the loose hair that hangs to the waist (in contrast to most renditions, which depict either short hair or long hair tied in a chongo knot). The figure is seated on a clay disc and is modeled in a light, buff-colored clay with chocolate brown and terra-cotta detailing.

Adobe Gallery, Albuquerque, New Mexico, 7 children, 6¼ inches high.

Figure 38. Rose Pecos-Sun Rhodes (Jemez), Female Navajo Storyteller, 1983

This artist from Jemez has been noted for her Navajo-style Storytellers. The figure shown here, modeled in light buff clay with chocolate brown and terra-cotta detailing, has five boys in cowboy hats and two girls holding Navajo baskets arranged on the extended skirt of the adult. The woman holds a baby in a traditional Navajo cradleboard, the top of which is just visible here behind the little boy holding a puppy.

Museum of Northern Arizona Gift Shop, Flagstaff, Arizona, 8 children, 5½ inches high.

colors, Carol's work frequently has accents of red, blue, and white. These colors are applied after firing, which is done in the traditional manner, "out in the open," at Jemez. Although she lived in Albuquerque in the mid-1980s, Carol and her husband maintained a home at Jemez and were active in Pueblo affairs. Carol has taught her children to make pottery and helped them with their Storytellers. In the late 1970s, her daughters (Rose, Jackie, and Stephanie), her son Irwin, and her daughter-in-law Jeanette all began to make figures. Rose has specialized in Navajo Storytellers painted in the traditional Jemez brown, beige, and terra-cotta polychrome. Instead of placing her figures on a clay disc, she has often extended the long skirt of a female Storyteller to form the base on which the children are placed (Figure 38).

Since the mid-1970s, yet another large Jemez family has produced prize-winning Storytellers. Like the Loretto sisters, the six daughters of potter Grace Fragua — Bonnie Fragua, Felicia Fragua, Rose T. Fragua, Emily F. Tsosie, Caroline Fragua Gachupin, and Cindy Fragua — have helped each other and frequently worked together. They have made a variety of figurative forms, but their "standard" Storytellers are very similar indeed. While Bonnie's prize-winning figures are much larger and more complex, they have much in common with her sister Caroline's, such as the squash-blossom necklace, the ceremonial painted circles on the face, and the textured hair (Figure 39). As Caroline has said, "She's dressed up for the Feast."

Her sister Emily Tsosie has made a wide variety of figures, but her clowns — both mudheads and koshares — have been the most popular and the most awarded of her figures. In the early 1980s, she won prizes at Gallup Ceremonial, Scottsdale, Eight Northern Pueblos, and Indian

> *"My husband, Sun Rhodes, who is an Arapaho, used to put his cowboy hat on our little son, and I wanted to capture that look in clay, but it did not fit in with the Pueblo style, so I started doing a Navajo version, with little boys in cowboy hats and little girls holding traditional Navajo wedding baskets. I make a point of putting in traditional Navajo cradleboards and the correct detailing on the little girls' sashes."*
>
> **Rose Pecos-Sun Rhodes**
> **Jemez**

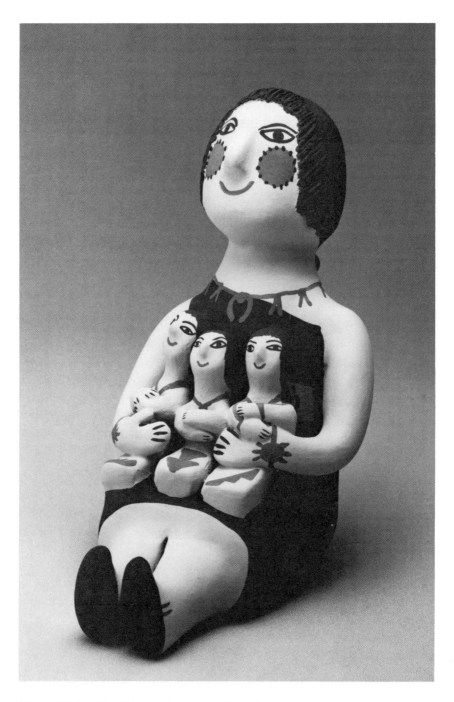

Figure 39. Caroline Fragua Gachupin (Jemez), Female Storyteller, 1981

Caroline's Storytellers often have ceremonial circles painted on the adult's cheeks and textured hair, which is smooth in back but modeled around the face. Here, the children have modeled noses; their feet are encased in blankets. The woman wears a simple manta, a squash-blossom necklace, and bracelets on both wrists. The figures are light buff, with black and terra-cotta detailing.

Adobe Gallery, Albuquerque, New Mexico, 3 children, 6½ inches high.

Market. In addition to Koshare Storytellers, such as the one on a Jemez-style disc shown in Color Plate 21, she has made scenes of clowns in action (for example, mudheads climbing out of a kiva) and has attached small clowns to turtles and other figures, as well as to bowls and wedding vases. Emily and other Jemez potters repeatedly told us that they preferred making figures to bowls and jars and wedding vases because they were "fun" to make and because they allowed them to experiment: "You can always do something different and it's never boring." Clearly, so many Jemez potters have become successful with Storytellers since 1978 because, among other reasons, they enjoy making them.

Tewa Pueblos

In addition to Tesuque and Santa Clara, the Tewa-speaking Pueblos long famous for their Rain Gods and *animalitos*, Storytellers and related figurines were being made at Nambe, San Juan, and San Ildefonso during the 1980s.

Tesuque. Long before the commercialization and popularization of Tesuque Rain Gods in the early decades of the twentieth century, potters from this Pueblo were producing a variety of figurines in addition to fine polychrome vessels. The earliest known figures collected by Col. James Stevenson and photographed by Ben Wittick between 1878 and 1881 were, like the later Rain Gods, small, seated, male and female figures of three types: (1) unpainted micaceous ware, (2) blackware, and (3) buff-slipped with black and red painted details.[58] (For examples of the third type, see the smaller figures in the foreground of Wittick photo, Figure 5.) Figures made after 1900 for tourists were less explicitly sexual, were rarely polished, and were slipped with white on which red and blue designs were painted. After the introduction of poster paints in the 1920s, Tesuque figures were made in a darker, tan, unpolished clay with a wide spectrum of brightly colored, painted designs.[59] Over the years Lorencita Pino, who began making pottery in 1916, has made all the different styles of Rain Gods — white painted with *guaco,* unpainted micaceous figures, and "regular Tesuque clay painted with acrylics." Between 1945 and 1950, she began making large Rain Gods with small children on them, and she continued to make them intermittently after that time.

Manuel Vigil's mother, Anastasia, also made Rain Gods in the early 1900s and, after Manuel lost a leg in a car accident in 1948, he joined his wife Vicenta in making them. He soon turned to modeling scenes of

Pueblo life similar to those made by Martin Vigil[60] in the 1920s, and he, too, won prizes for them at Indian Market. With the exception of some micaceous figures, all of Manuel's figures have been brightly painted after firing and frequently clothed with cloth, rabbit fur, and feathers. In 1959, Manuel made the first of the countless Nativities[61] for which he later became famous. He made the first of his unique interpretations of the Storyteller about 1977. Vigil's Storytellers are unmistakable, with their bright colors, children almost as big as the storyteller, and rabbit-fur hair (Color Plate 22).

Nambe. Although once known for its polychrome and various types of utility ware, Nambe Pueblo produced very little pottery after the turn of the century. In the early 1980s, Virginia Gutierrez, a native of Nambe who moved to Pojoaque, and her sisters, Emiliana Gadd Vigil and Marie Herrera, both from Nambe, produced a variety of ceramic figures, including Storytellers, in addition to small jars and wedding vases. Marie has made micaceous cooking pots and has frequently added some micaceous paint to her polychrome Storytellers, as can be seen on the shoulder blanket of the storyteller in Figure 40.

San Juan. Reycita Garcia was the only major potter producing figurines in her native village of San Juan in the mid-1980s. She learned as a child to make the traditional San Juan red-on-tan and incised ware from her mother, and until about 1955 made mostly bowls and jars. Her first figure, which she has called a "Storyteller," was a small mother and child similar to the one shown in Figure 41. She went on to make and win prizes for many more Storytellers (male and female), Corn Grinders, Drummers, and Nativities.[62] Her red-and-white-on-tan fig-

> *"In the wintertime my seven brothers and sisters and I would sit around the fire eating parched corn or piñon or sunflower seeds, and our father, Onofre Vigil, would tell us stories. I cannot remember all of them, but I do remember the serpent story: there was a terrible flood, and water was pouring over our land, and the people didn't know where to run. Then the serpent laid its body across the falls and stopped the water, saving the people. At Nambe Falls Dam, if the water level is not too high, you can still see the serpent; it's as if it's painted on the rock."*
>
> **Marie Herrera**
> **Nambe**

Figure 40. Marie Herrera (Nambe), Male Storyteller, 1984

This male Storyteller (along with a female companion piece) is modeled in red clay with detailing in black, white, and terra-cotta. Arrayed in a sparkling shoulder blanket of micaceous clay, he wears red boots because, as the artist explained, "For ceremonial dances the men wear red moccasins." The facial features in Marie's figurative art are indicated with just a touch of modeling. "I don't like anything too perfect." She signs her pieces simply, "Marie, Nambe," with the date.

Artist's Collection, Nambe, New Mexico, 6 children, 7 inches high.

ures, with their incised features, are well crafted and unmistakably San Juan style.

San Ildefonso. Long famous for its polychrome and black-on-red ware, San Ildefonso became the most famous of pottery-making Pueblos, as the home of Maria and Julian Martinez and of the distinctive black-on-black (matte paint on a polished surface) pottery which they discovered in 1919. Figurative pottery, however, was not part of the San Ildefonso tradition or of the ceramics revival initiated by Maria. With the exception of decorated and incised blackware and redware bears produced by Maria's grandson, Tony Da, a few interesting clown and dancer figures made by the late Enke Pena, and Alfred Aguilar's blackware buffalos, no figures of note were produced at San Ildefonso before 1975, and relatively few had appeared by the mid-1980s.

The most prolific of San Ildefonso's figurative potters, Alfred Aguilar ("Sä Wä Pin"), first made Nativities[63] and Storytellers about 1975. The variety of textures, colors, and forms in his figures is quite unique and understandably award-winning, as evidenced in the "Hunter's Storyteller" scene illustrated in Color Plate 23. His brother, Jose V. Aguilar, Sr. ("Yellowbird"), has also made a variety of Storytellers and other prize-winning figures, all in black-on-black. Juan Tafoya has not made Storytellers, but he, too, has won prizes during the 1980s for his blackware figures. Occasionally, world-famous potter Blue Corn has shaped figures instead of vessels in her distinctive polychrome, such as a Corn Grinder that was awarded a second prize at the 1980 Indian Market.

Santa Clara. At least since 1879, when Col. James Stevenson collected pottery there, the Pueblo of Santa Clara has produced polished blackware figurines as well as large vessels. As the size of the vessels decreased in response to tourist taste after the turn of the century, the number of small, nontraditional forms and *animalitos* increased. Whatever else they made and whatever new paints and designs were

> *"I make them [my figures] from the Mother Earth clay and also the paints from the earth colors. For modeling I just use several toothpicks and a popsicle stick; these are my only tools, other than my nimble fingers. I fire them outside."*
>
> **Reycita Garcia**
> **San Juan**

Figure 41. Reycita Garcia (San Juan), Female Storyteller, ca.1974

In the mid-1980s, Reycita Garcia was the only artist in San Juan working consistently in figurative ceramics. Her distinctive style includes minimal detailing of both figures and facial features, which are incised and modeled, rather than painted. The woman's white hair is worn in the customary chongo knot, but with stylized, spiky bangs — an unusual touch. Reycita uses the warm, tan-colored clay of her Pueblo, with red and white clay paints.

Barbara Weigand Collection, Santa Fe, New Mexico, 1 child, 4½ inches high.

introduced, Santa Clara potters continued, for over three-quarters of a century, to shape appealing, minimally modeled, high-quality figurines, ranging in size from one to twelve inches. After 1964, when Maria I. Naranjo began making Nativities, and after 1968, when she made the first Santa Clara Storyteller, several well-known potters in this Pueblo began to make human as well as animal figures, and their *animalitos* grew into Storyteller animals.

Already famous for her prize-winning *animalitos*, Maria I. Naranjo was the first Pueblo artist to make a matte-and-polished blackware Nativity in 1965. Later, she made redware Nativities as well as Nativities that are a combination of red, black, tan, and gray polished and matte figures.[64] She used this same unusual and distinctive combination in the 1981 Storyteller illustrated in Color Plate 24. Maria made her first Storyteller in 1968 in response to a friend's request and has shaped many others in redware and blackware, in addition to her later polychrome style. As Doris Monthan has noted, these very abstract, matte-and-polished figures "have the quality of fine sculpture and have won numerous awards."[65] In the late 1970s, her daughter, Martha Mirabal, began to produce superb miniature Nativities and Storytellers in the same style and encouraged her son and daughter to make *animalitos* and other miniature figures.

Husband-and-wife team Dorothy and Paul Gutierrez have also made fine and distinctive redware and blackware Nativities and Storytellers. They began making pottery in 1965 with assistance and instruction from Paul's aunt, Margaret Gutierrez, and his sister, Pauline Naranjo. They made their first Nativities[66] in 1971 and after 1972 began to win prizes for these and other figures at major shows throughout the Southwest. In 1976, Dorothy and Paul began making miniature mudheads and in 1978 were the first to create Storyteller Mudheads. A few of these are in redware, but most, ranging in size from two to ten inches, are matte blackware with polished details (Color Plate 25).

Paul's aunt, Margaret, and his father, Luther Gutierrez, began working as a team in 1966, continuing the intricately designed, unusual pastel polychrome developed and perfected by their parents, Lela and Van Gutierrez, between 1905 and 1966. Internationally known and awarded for their pottery vessels and their Disney-like *animalitos*, Margaret and Luther first produced Nativities[67] and animal Storytellers in 1978. Since then they have created an array of animal and human Storytellers — frogs, raccoons, bears, Pueblo mothers, mudheads, and koshares. The Koshare Storyteller illustrated in Color Plate 26 is a unique interpretation of this popular Pueblo figure with his cornhusk horns and obvious sense of humor.

In the early 1980s, many other Santa Clara potters — such as Marie Askan, Linda Halsey, Crescencia Tafoya, and Flora, Joe, Madeline, and Pauline Naranjo — produced prize-winning figurines of varieties other than Storytellers. One of the most prolific and, certainly, the most innovative of Santa Clara figurative potters during the 1980s has been Nora Naranjo-Morse. Her anthropomorphic figures, which have an abstract quality that is both very modern and very primitive, collected ten "Non-Traditional" prizes at Indian Market alone between 1979 and 1984. Each of her unique and humorous figures has a story and a name, such as her autobiographical "Me and the Twins" figure.[68]

Tiwa Pueblos

Unlike some of their Tewa-speaking neighbors, the northern Tiwa Pueblos (Taos and Picuris), have never produced much painted pottery. Tiwa pottery is primarily unslipped and unpainted cooking ware made of micaceous clay and once produced in abundance at Picuris. A few small human and animal figures produced over the years at Taos and Picuris have been made in this same style. As Frank Harlow pointed out in 1977, "When James Stevenson visited the famous Pueblo of Taos in about 1880, he found that pottery making had nearly ceased. In the intervening years, there have been no serious attempts at revival of this venerable craft, although a few potters still produce a small output."[69]

Taos. The Storytellers, Mudhead Clowns, and Nativities that appeared at Taos Pueblo in the 1970s and early 1980s were made by Jemez potters who had married into the Pueblo. Alma Concha Loretto (see Jemez section) began making Storytellers and Nativities after she moved to Taos in 1969. In addition to teaching her own children, she also assisted Juanita Martinez, who first tried a Storyteller in 1979. By 1984 Alma had moved back to Jemez, but Juanita was still living and working in Taos where she used Jemez clays and paints and fired inside in her woodstove. She has won prizes for her black, buff, and terra-cotta Nativities as well as her Storytellers, which are distinguished by their elongated style and their Taos braids (Figure 42); her two teenage daughters have also made Storytellers. Another Taos potter, Bernie Naranjo, began to make very interesting, large, unpainted, micaceous figures in the 1980s, but he did not make Storytellers.

Figure 42. Juanita Martinez (Taos), Male Storyteller, 1983

A native of Jemez, Juanita moved to Taos Pueblo when she married. She made her first Storyteller in 1979, inspired by Alma Concha, another Jemez native who lived in Taos at that time. She continued to use Jemez clays and paints; her male Storyteller here is modeled in buff-colored clay, with painted terra-cotta clothes and black accents. Three of the boys are holding balls, one holds a drum, and another, a bird. Juanita's figures are easily recognized by their long torsos, large, oval-shaped mouths, and Taos-style braids. After her figures are painted they are fired in the woodstove in her living room.

Adobe Gallery, Albuquerque, New Mexico, 14 children, 8½ inches high.

Isleta. The southernmost Tiwa Pueblo, Isleta, never produced much pottery. Most of the small, tourist-market vessels made around the turn of the century and sometimes called Isleta Polychrome were, in fact, made by Laguna Indians who moved to Isleta about 1880. Stella Teller, from one of the few pottery-making families in Isleta, has consistently won prizes for her Storytellers and Nativities since she made the first one in 1978. Her great-grandmother Marcellina Jojolla, her grandmother Emelia Lente Carpio, and her mother, Felicita Jojolla, were all potters. Stella learned from her mother, who made only small pots, when she was a child and made little bears and dogs that sold for fifteen cents. In 1962, she began making pottery steadily and soon became known for making much larger and finer bowls, jars, and wedding vases than had been produced at Isleta in many decades; in the mid-1980s, she won numerous prizes for these traditional shapes. Stella's pottery is distinguished by its subtle and unusual colors, which are all natural. The light gray which has become her trademark is produced by mixing white clay with manganese. She was the first and one of the very few potters to embed turquoise stones into the clay, as can be seen in the belt and necklace of the Navajo Storyteller featured in Color Plate 27. In addition to Navajo Storytellers distinguished by their dark and light gray paint, Stella has made Isleta Storytellers dressed in mantas and distinctive lace blouses, Taos Storytellers with striped blankets, and Apache Storytellers with fringed and beaded dresses and babies in cradleboards. When not working full time at the Indian Pueblo Cultural Center in Albuquerque, Stella has continued to experiment with different sizes and types of Storytellers and has been joined in doing so by her three daughters, Chris Lucero, Ramona Blythe, and Lynette Teller.

"My cousin and I often went out in the wagon with my grandfather to cut wheat or hoe in the cornfields, and, while we were riding along or working in the fields, he would tell us stories. Across the river my grandmother would be cooking beans and tortillas in the summer house, and it smelled so good. At the times when we worked in silence, I would dream of becoming a good potter some day."

Juanita Martinez
Taos

Figure 43. Nellie Bica (Zuni), Owl Storyteller, 1980-1981

This highly stylized mother owl and the baby on each wing all have identical patterning and looped beaks. They are fashioned in clay from Nutria (on the Zuni Reservation, about twenty miles northeast of the village). In contrast to the gray surface and black painted details of most animal figures from Cochiti Pueblo, this Zuni Storyteller is cream-colored with brown and terra-cotta detailing. The figure is signed "N.B. Zuni."

The Kiva Indian Trading Post, Santa Fe, New Mexico, 2 babies, 7 inches high.

> "My mother's youngest sister taught me when I was in my teens [ca. 1917]. Owls were the first potteries I made. That's the way they taught them in those days. I always put babies on my owls, and I think I was one of the first to make owls with legs. Now my daughter and three granddaughters make them, too."
>
> **Nellie Bica**
> **Zuni**

Zuni Pueblo

The longest documented tradition of historic figurative ceramic design, both painted and modeled, exists at the western-most New Mexico Pueblo of Zuni. F. W. Hodge excavated human and animal figurines and effigy vessels that were made at Hawikuh between 1475 and 1680; in 1879, Col. James Stevenson purchased many of the same sorts of representational figures from Zuni potters. The most popular figurative forms in the Stevenson collection were birds, especially owls. Among these were several composite figures: an owl "bearing the young owls on its back" (see Figure 4) and a "hen with three young chickens on her back."[70] Zuni potters continued to make similar figures in the twentieth century and by the 1920s, the owl had become a standard tourist item.

Since then, as Margaret Hardin has pointed out, "it would seem that every potter has made owls," but "everyone's owls are different."[71] During the 1970s and 1980s, fine single as well as composite owls with baby owls were produced by Myra Eriacho, Jenny Laate, Josephine Nahohai, Anderson Peynetsa, and Nellie Bica (who has also taught her daughter and three granddaughters to make pottery). Nellie learned to make pottery by making owls about 1917 and has continued making them into the mid-1980s. Her owls always have babies on them and some of them are footed (see Figure 4, from the Stevenson collection); others, modeled without feet (Figure 43), resemble effigy jars made centuries ago. Cochiti and Acoma potters have often referred to their very similar composite owls (see Figures 22 and 28) as "Storyteller Owls" or simply "Storytellers," and Anglo buyers and sellers have frequently described Zuni owls as "Storytellers," but Zuni potters have told us that they are not Storytellers but simply "an owl (*muhukwi*) with her children." Nonetheless, like Singing Mothers and Storytellers, a Zuni owl with its children is also an image of reproduction, of life continuing, and the pottery form itself has been a vehicle of Pueblo cultural continuity for over a century.

The Regenerative Power of the Storyteller

 There is little doubt that the Storyteller is a powerful generative image, capable of endlessly reproducing itself. The process of reproduction has not been limited, however, to almost two hundred Pueblo potters producing Storytellers of all sizes, shapes, and colors for sale to an Anglo market. The Anglo art world has also reproduced Storytellers in a variety of media. Photographic reproductions of pottery Storytellers, principally Helen Cordero's, have been used on notecards and Christmas cards sold by southwestern museums and by UNICEF, on calendars produced both by UNICEF and *American Indian Art* magazine, on posters printed by The Hand and the Spirit Gallery and the Colorado Springs Symphony, and (as line drawings of Rain Gods once were) in countless advertisements for Indian art shops and galleries. In the mid-1980s, a shop called The Storyteller Indian Arts Gallery opened in Santa Fe. Assorted, two-dimensional Anglo renditions of Storytellers have also appeared, not only on notecards and stationery, but as needlepoint designs, silk-screens, ceramic tiles, and even on T-shirts sold as of 1984 at a Santa Fe curio shop.

Helen Cordero never dreamed that her "little people" would come to life in such abundant and varied forms, and her response to this phenomenon has been somewhat ambivalent. While she has recognized that imitation is a form of flattery and that she has done something very important in terms of contemporary Pueblo ceramics, she has not liked the endless reproduction of something so very personal and autobiographical: "They call them Storytellers, but they don't even know what it means. They don't know it's my grandfather." Nor has she liked the fact that more potters than will admit have not made their Storytellers in a traditional manner and have used commercial clays, paints, and kilns: "Today, everything is easy. Buy their clay, their paint, take them to big ovens in Albuquerque. Grandma Clay doesn't like it and most of them don't even know about Grandma Clay. To make good potteries you have to do it the right way, the old way, and you have to have a special, happy feeling inside."

Clearly, Helen did something right, or almost two hundred other potters would not have begun doing the same thing. But, contrary to what Helen's remarks imply, the overwhelming majority of potters *have* made their Storytellers "in the old way." In fact, both the popularity of the Storyteller and the efforts of Marie Romero have contributed to a notable revival of traditional materials and techniques at Jemez, where, among the hundreds of figures produced in the mid-1980s, one would be hard-pressed to find "garish trinkets." Whatever the reasons these other potters have had for making Storytellers and related figures, and however they do it, there is no question that during the 1970s and the 1980s there was a new and flourishing genre of Pueblo pottery and a new valuation and revaluation of figurative ceramics among dealers and collectors.

The repertoire of figurative forms produced by New Mexico potters has been enormous and impressive in the range of shapes, sizes, skill, and prices represented. Each year the number and types of other figures have increased along with new variations in the style, shape, and substance of the Storyteller. Since 1978, I have seen the pattern of innovation and imitation repeated again and again. A telling case in point is the Navajo Storyteller, first made by Isleta potter Stella Teller in 1981. Since then, this figure — in which the storyteller's skirt extends out to form a base on which the children are placed — has been imitated by many Jemez potters, and in 1984, Helen Cordero shaped the first Cochiti Navajo Storyteller. It is quite likely that in the future many other potters at Cochiti and elsewhere will add a Navajo Storyteller to their repertoires. The same thing happened with animal Storytellers after Cochiti and Acoma potters began re-inventing the Zuni owl and other composite animal forms, and Santa Clara *animal-itos* became Storyteller animals in the late 1970s. In 1974 there were no Storyteller animals; in 1986, they were everywhere.

Traditional Storytellers or Singing Mothers were unquestionably the most popular composite figures made in the mid-1980s throughout the Pueblos. However, in keeping with the pattern of community specialization, different Pueblos distinguished themselves for particular variations of the Storyteller or for particular figures other than Storytellers. At Santa Clara, for example, animal and clown Storytellers were the most popular forms, and only in this Pueblo could one find matte-and-polished blackware and redware Storytellers. Tesuque, long-famous for its poster-paint Rain Gods, produced brightly colored Storytellers which were very much the exception at other Pueblos. The red, buff, and incised figures made by Reycita Garcia were unique in her Pueblo, but unmistakably and characteristically San Juan style. In addition to reviving the owl and other bird forms for which they have long been famous, Acoma potters have tended to specialize in effigy-style Storytellers in particular and in combining figurative and vessel forms in general. Many of their Storytellers incorporate one or more small pots, and many bowls, jars, and wedding vases are appliquéd with small figures. Jemez Storytellers are distinguished not only by their dark tan slip and brown paint, but by the distinctive disc on which the storyteller or storytelling scene is placed. In the early 1980s, miniatures became very popular with Jemez potters, who began to produce more miniature Storytellers than any other Pueblo. The most popular variation at Jemez, in substance as well as style, was the clown figure. Here, as at Santa Clara, both koshares and mudheads were shaped in abundance — notably by Maxine Toya, Alma Concha, and Emily Tsosie. At the same time, Jemez potters also began making a variety of animal Storytellers, and in 1982 Caroline and Santana Seonia displayed the first of their "Storyteller" Balloons at the Eight Northern Pueblos Fair. Given Albuquerque's fame as "Balloon Capital" of the world, this innovation, too, seems destined for reproduction.

Other than Storytellers and the Singing Mothers that they had been making for decades, the most popular single figure with Helen Cordero and other Cochiti potters in the mid-1980s was the Drummer. Cochiti has long been famous among the Pueblos for its fine drums, made for and sold both to other Pueblos for ceremonial use and to Anglos for decorative purposes. Many potters' husbands have sold drums and won prizes for them, and the drum, like the Storyteller, has become an important symbol of community identity: the Cochiti landscape is dominated by two water towers painted to look like drums, and the end of every pew in the Pueblo's St. Bonaventura Church is decorated with an incised drum. Small seated and standing ceramic Drummers were made at Cochiti as early as the 1950s, and they, too, became much larger and more numerous in the 1970s and 1980s. Among the animal Storytellers made at Cochiti, owls, frogs, and turtles were the most popular. Louis Naranjo's bears were widely known and distributed, but as of 1985, he was the only potter making them. If the revived tradition of portraits of whitemen becomes increasingly popular with Anglo consumers in the future, it seems quite likely that other Cochiti potters will join Louis Naranjo and Ivan Lewis in producing caricature figures.

Josephine Arquero did so in the mid-1980s with a few cowboys and priests, and potters in other Pueblos will probably follow suit.

As Guy and Doris Monthan documented in *Nacimientos* (1979) and, as our subsequent investigations have further revealed, almost all figurative potters have tried their hands at Nativities, encouraged in the 1980s by Adobe Gallery's annual Christmas Nativity Show. While many potters in all the figurative-pottery-making Pueblos except Zuni have made Nativities, these have not been the most popular figures produced. Nativities take more time and effort to make than single figures, are more difficult to package and transport, and inevitably have a higher price tag, which means that they don't sell as quickly. In response to this situation, a number of potters, particularly at Cochiti, Jemez, and Santa Clara, began making either miniature Nativities or minimal, three-piece ones. Nonetheless, the Nativity was a favorite form with both producers and consumers in the 1980s, and it will probably continue to be an important subject in the repertoire of figurative ceramics.

By 1986 there were at least three generations of Pueblo figurative ceramists and there was no reason to assume that this revival would not continue. The third generation of children and teenagers making Storytellers seemed to "increase by magic." Every time we returned to the Pueblos or went to a gallery or Indian art fair, there was yet another daughter, granddaughter, or grandson "starting up" and "getting real good." Many of the second generation of middle-aged potters learned, as their children did later, to make pottery by shaping Storytellers. After mastering this form and producing prize-winning Storytellers and Nativities in the 1970s and 1980s, they began to experiment, to revive older ceramic styles, and to learn how to make traditional vessels. In contrast, the first generation mothers or aunts, such as Damacia Cordero or Persingula Gachupin, who had taught their children to use the clay and who had spent their lives making bowls and jars or figures that sold for very little, were beginning to "have fun" trying their skills at Storytellers and to enjoy at last the pleasure of being paid for their talents.

When asked why they made Storytellers or how they came to make them, many potters responded that the design appealed and offered an interesting alternative to bowls and jars, that a friend or relative was making them and one day they decided to try it, that they discovered they were good at making figures and enjoyed the fun and the freedom of modeling. Another obvious, but less frequently stated, factor has been the ready market of dealers and collectors and tourists. A small Storyteller is not only more fun to make than a small bowl, it has also been much more likely to sell, both to children and their parents.

Almost without exception, Storyteller potters told us about the grandmother or grandfather or aunt or uncle who had told them stories, and then they told us these stories yet again. These retellings bespeak an involvement with tradition far more basic than patrons' interest in archaic patterns or appealing images of Pueblo life. In the words of Acoma poet, Simon Ortiz, "the only way to continue is to tell a story and there is no other way."[72] And in her novel about Pueblo life, *Ceremony*, Leslie Silko has also told us that "stories are life for the people" and "you don't have anything if you don't have the stories."[73] Pueblo stories were and are one of the primary modes in which the family, the clan, and the community regenerate themselves, for stories both describe and create "chains" linking generation to generation and back again, and embody a vital dynamic of "bringing and keeping the people together" and of endless creation, for each story is the beginning of many stories, a "seed of seeds."[74]

As conceived by Helen Cordero, the clay Storyteller is itself the material expression of regeneration: the very structure of this large figure alive with small children re-enacts this reproductive dynamic; its proportions are, indeed, social proportions; and its subject is explicitly relationship — between generations, between past and future, and between words and things. "We are," as she has said, "all in there, in the clay." From the Pueblo point of view, stories and potteries — like kinship systems — constitute a "bridge between the reproductive aspect of generation and the cultural basis of thought, transmission."[75] Both are vital necessities, conceived in terms of and themselves expressions of natality. Like telling stories, making and exchanging potteries has always been a vehicle for retelling family history and for expressing personal and tribal identity. With the encroachment of an Anglo world and the expansion of an Anglo market for Indian objects, ceramic art has become increasingly important, not only as a source of income, but as a cultural voice. Helen Cordero's first Storyteller has engendered countless "little people," her own and others', because, among other things, it celebrates the things of ordinary Pueblo experience and speaks in terms of these cultural constants — stories, generations, and the persistent problem of community organization and survival. Like the subjects which they represent, Storytellers themselves have become a significant means of bringing and keeping Pueblo people together.

BARBARA A. BABCOCK

PART II

Color Plates

Colors of the Storyteller

The plates which follow illustrate one of the more interesting and quintessential aspects of the Storyteller revolution — the ways in which the polychrome prototype created by Helen Cordero of Cochiti has been translated by potters in thirteen other New Mexico Pueblos into the clays, paints, and designs traditionally associated with each Pueblo. "Stylistic screens" are well established and well developed among pottery-producing Pueblos, and, despite a thousand years of trading, borrowing, and intermarriage, there are marked stylistic boundaries that both potters and ceramic specialists recognize. Within the characteristic regional styles associated with one or more Pueblos, one frequently finds further variations peculiar to extended pottery-producing families, such as the Loretto sisters from Jemez and their children, as well as the idiosyncratic variations of innovative individuals, such as Stella Teller of Isleta. The many different colors of Pueblo Storytellers produced in the 1980s vary in relation to both materials and methods — the clays from which they are shaped; the mineral, vegetal, or commercial substances with which they are painted; and the manner in which they are fired — which are influenced both by the Pueblo of birth and apprenticeship and by the Pueblo of residence.

Black and terra-cotta designs on a cream-colored slip have characterized Cochiti polychrome for over a century. From a Singing Mother made in the 1870s (Plate 1) to Singing Mothers and Storytellers made by Helen Cordero (Plates 2–6) and other Cochiti potters (e.g., Plates 7 and 10) between 1960 and 1985, the colors of Cochiti figures have varied little. The white slip and terra-cotta paint are mineral paints made by mixing locally gathered clays with water. The black paint or *guaco* is a vegetal paint produced by boiling Rocky Mountain beeweed into a sludge that is allowed to harden into a cake used like water colors. Except for the substitution of commercial paintbrushes for those made of yucca, the materials and methods as well as the colors and styles of ceramic decoration have remained unchanged for decades. As figurative production increased after the late 1960s, subtle variations, such as changes in color proportion, began to appear within this stylistic consistency. Much larger areas of black or terra-cotta in relation to cream are quite marked in the figures that Helen Cordero made after the mid-1970s (compare Plate 6 with Plates 2–5); the Mudhead Storytellers that Tony Dallas shaped in the 1980s are primarily terra-cotta (see Figure 26), while Louis Naranjo's Storyteller Bears are predominantly black (Plate 9). Ada Suina's polychrome designs are distinguished by the addition of a fourth color, a pale apricot clay paint (Plate 8). Dorothy Trujillo, originally from Jemez Pueblo, has used Cochiti clays and paints, but has produced a noticeably darker buff or light tan slip that is more characteristic of Jemez (Plate 11). By the early 1980s, several Cochiti potters, notably Vangie Suina (see Figure 27), were using acrylic paints and kiln-firing, producing a much brighter, glossier, and whiter polychrome. Firing in a gas or electric or wood-fueled kiln — the last type created by cutting an oil drum in half — produces different colors (even when natural paints are used) than does the open-grate, cow-manure method and eliminates the gray or "smoked" cast of traditionally fired polychrome.

In contrast to the bentonite clays used by Cochiti potters, Acoma potters use a kaolin clay, which requires a mineral black paint. For many decades, Acoma polychrome has been distinguished by its stark white kaolin slip and its fine-line, black designs, represented here in the figures of Frances Torivio Pino, Ethel Shields, and Marilyn Henderson (Plates 12–14). By the 1980s, many Acoma potters were, as Marilyn Henderson has admitted, kiln-firing, making for an even chalkier white surface. The variety of styles and colors found in the Storytellers of other Keres Pueblos reflects both the potter's natal Pueblo and family influence. Lupe Lucero of San Felipe, one of the six Loretto sisters from Jemez, has continued to use Jemez clays and paints, and her work (Plate 15) is exclusively in the buff and terra-cotta combination used by her sisters Alma Concha Loretto and Fannie Wall Loretto (see Figures 35 and 36).

Jemez pottery in general is much browner than that of other Pueblos. Many of the Storytellers produced in this Pueblo are distinguished by a tan slip and dark brown as well as black and terra-cotta painted designs (see, in particular, Plates 16, 17, and 21). The figures of Carol Pecos, however, are personalized by the addition of red, blue, and white accents after firing (Plate 20). While Alma Concha Loretto's Taos-style Storytellers are entirely buff and terra-cotta (see Figure 35), her Mudhead Storytellers reverse the proportion of these two colors and incorporate black details (Plate 18). Her sisters Edna Coriz of Santo Domingo and Mary E. Toya of Jemez (Plate 19) have both painted their Storytellers in a more traditional buff, terra-cotta, and black polychrome. The work of Mary's seven children is also in this style.

In the 1920s, Tesuque potters began making their "Rain Gods" in unpolished tan clay which they "garishly" painted after firing with poster-paint colors. Manuel Vigil has continued this tradition in his unmistakable Storytellers, which are painted in bright, primary colors of Bisque stain (Plate 22). The Storytellers of Alfred Aguilar of San Ildefonso Pueblo (Plate 23) are equally distinctive, painted in an unusual variety of natural colors, in marked contrast to the characteristic black-on-black figures produced by his brother, Jose V. Aguilar, Sr., and several other potters in this Pueblo. For at least a century, artists of Santa Clara Pueblo have also produced matte-and-polished blackware figures by firing them in a reducing atmosphere. In the 1980s, several potters, notably Dorothy and Paul Gutierrez, were producing Storytellers in this style (Plate 25). In addition to making Storytellers in the black-on-black and red-on-red ware for which Santa Clara is famous, Maria I. Naranjo has developed a unique combination of red, black, tan, and gray matte-and-polished finish for her Nativities and Storytellers (Plate 24). The most unusual Santa Clara Storytellers have been created by Margaret and Luther Gutierrez (Plate 26). Their Disneylike figures are painted in the unusual pastel polychrome developed and perfected by their parents, Lela and Van Gutierrez, between 1905 and 1966.

The Tiwa Pueblos have never been major decorative pottery-producing centers, but that may well change as the number of figurative potters at Taos and Isleta increases. Isleta potter Stella Teller, in particular, has developed a unique style and combination of subtle natural colors. The light gray, which has become her trademark, is made by mixing manganese with white clay and is used in one of her Navajo Storytellers (Plate 27).

The twenty-seven color plates in this section represent the work of twenty-three potters from eight of the fourteen Storyteller-producing Pueblos, presented in the order in which Pueblos and potters are discussed in the text of Part I.

Plate 1. Mother and Child Effigy (Cochiti), 1875–1880

This small, polychrome figure — collected by Sheldon Jackson in the late 1870s — is the earliest known Cochiti Singing Mother and in all probability was purchased from Jake Gold. The mother's dress is painted front and back with corn plant designs. Her hands, feet, and mouth, and the baby she is holding are painted with micaceous terra-cotta.

Museum of Natural History, Princeton University, Acc. No. P.U. 7757, 7 inches high.

93

Plate 2. Helen Cordero (Cochiti), Singing Mother, 1960–1961

This figure is characteristic of the many small figures made by Helen Cordero between 1959 and 1963 and is very similar to those made by other Cochiti potters between 1920 and 1960. Like many figures produced by Helen in her first decade of pottery making, this Singing Mother is minimally sanded and slipped, and the surface is rather rough. Also typical of this period in Helen's career is the large amount of cream slip surface with minimal black and terra-cotta painted design. Already evident are the intricate and careful details in the woman's clothing, characteristic of Helen's later fine work.

Marjorie Lambert Collection, Santa Fe, New Mexico, 5½ inches high.

Plate 3. Helen Cordero (Cochiti), The First Storyteller, 1964

The first Storyteller, made for Alexander Girard in 1964, was the beginning of a new
genre of Pueblo pottery. The adult figure here has open eyes, but in subsequent
interpretations their eyes are always closed, as Helen has said, "because they're
thinking." She has varied the number of children on succeeding pieces and has placed
as many as thirty children on one figure. Despite later changes and refinements, this
original Storyteller's charisma appealed to the public immediately, presaging the
unparalleled success of both the theme and Helen's artistry. This figure has been
featured in Girard's 1968 exhibit and catalog, *The Magic of a People*, and on the cover
of *American Indian Art* (Spring 1983).

Museum of International Folk Art, Acc. No. A.79.53-41, Museum of New Mexico,
Santa Fe, 5 children, 8 inches high.

"When people ask me what it is, I tell them it's my grandfather. He's giving me these. His eyes are closed because he's thinking and his mouth is open because he's telling stories. That one, he was a really wise man. He knew so much and he was a really good storyteller. There were always lots of us grandchildrens around him, and we're all in there, in the clay."

"When I make a big piece like this that I know is going to a show and lots of people are going to see him, I talk to him and I tell him that. I tell him he has to come out real pretty, that he's going to go far away and be famous. If he doesn't come out, I'm sad, but I take him back into my heart and I make him again."

"I don't know why people go for my work the way they do. Maybe it's because to me they aren't just pretty things that I make for money. All my potteries come out of my heart. They're my little people. I talk to them and they're singing. If you're listening, you can hear them."

Helen Cordero
Cochiti

Plate 4. Helen Cordero (Cochiti), Male Storyteller, 1969–1970

Made five to six years after Helen's first Storyteller, this figure illustrates many refinements in modeling, sanding, and painting, as well as more careful and complex detailing. Despite the increased number of children, each child has a different facial expression, body position, and costume. The body of the adult figure is taller and better proportioned, and his face has assumed the expression that became Helen's trademark: his head is tilted back, eyes closed, and mouth open.

Katherine H. Rust Children's Collection, Albuquerque, New Mexico, 19 children, 11½ inches high.

Plate 5. Helen Cordero (Cochiti), Male Storyteller, 1971

By the early 1970s, Helen had established her unique style and had begun signing her pieces in *guaco*. This particular piece became quite famous. It took first prize at the 1971 Indian Market, was included in the 1975 book, *Art and Indian Individualists*, and in an article on Helen in the 1977 pottery issue of *American Indian Art*. In September 1976, it was featured on a poster for Helen's one-woman show at the Heard Museum in Phoenix, and in November 1982, it appeared on the cover of *National Geographic* magazine.

The Hand and the Spirit Crafts Gallery, Scottsdale, Arizona, 17 children, 12½ inches high.

Plate 6. Helen Cordero (Cochiti), "The Children's Hour," 1973

In this departure from her usual Storyteller, Helen separates the children from the adult figure. As she has explained: "These are older kids listening to him." Here there are five children, but there can be any number and they can be grouped at will. The adult figure is similar to several of her Pueblo Father figures. A novel feature of this piece is that the adult's pointed hat and clay cigarette are removable. Helen invented "The Children's Hour" in 1971, and the first time she "showed it out" at the Heard Museum's Indian Arts and Crafts Show, it was awarded a blue ribbon.

D and J Investment Company Collection, Phoenix, Arizona, 5 children, 10½ inches high.

Plate 7. Mary Trujillo (Cochiti), Female Storyteller, 1980–1981

A native of San Juan, the artist completed this piece within her first year of making Storytellers in Cochiti. In 1982, when she entered the Indian Market for the first time, one of her pieces ("Corn Husking Party") took first prize in its category and won the Katherine and Miguel Ortero Creative Excellence Award, an overall award for the entire market. This female Storyteller has a black manta over a feast-day dress and a patterned shawl over her shoulders, with one of the children peeking out of it.

Packard's Indian Trading Company, Santa Fe, New Mexico, 4 children, 8½ inches high.

Plate 8. Ada Suina (Cochiti), Male Storyteller, 1982

The granddaughter of the distinguished potter Estephanita Herrera, Ada Suina did not start making pottery until her mid-forties. This male Storyteller illustrates a number of her characteristic touches in both modeled and painted detail, including the addition of a fourth color — the pale orange slip, made from a special clay which is light yellow before firing. This color is used here for the adult's trousers and combined with the terra-cotta in some of the children's clothes.

Packard's Indian Trading Company, Santa Fe, New Mexico, 6 children, 9 inches high.

Plate 9. Louis Naranjo (Cochiti), Bear Storyteller, 1981

Son of famous Cochiti potter Frances Naranjo Suina, Louis learned to make Storytellers by observing his mother's work. However, he says, "My Bear Storytellers are my own creation." The seated adult shown here holds three cubs, and, as in all of this potter's interpretations of the theme, the adult is black and the cubs terra-cotta, with cream detailing for smaller areas. Louis's Bear Storytellers range from three to fifteen inches in height and have from one to five cubs; some adult bears are shown on all fours with the cubs on their backs.

The Kiva Indian Trading Post, Santa Fe, New Mexico, 3 babies, 8 inches high.

Plate 10. Felipa Trujillo (Cochiti), Female Storyteller, 1980

Among the first Cochiti potters to make Storytellers, Felipa began them in the mid-1960s. The female Storyteller shown here illustrates one of her trademarks — the baby in the cradleboard (which is also a distinctive feature in her Nativities). Other characteristic features are the modeled noses on both adult and children. Her figures have an even, light, cream-colored slip, which enhances the richness of the black and terra-cotta detailing. One of Felipa's earlier, male Storytellers, in a somewhat different style, is shown in Figure 11.

Adobe Gallery, Albuquerque, New Mexico, 5 children, 8½ inches high.

"Every time I build a figure, it is my grandfather I see, Jose La Luz Cata, of San Juan. I make a figure with braids because my grandfather wore braids, and I put a big hat on some because he always wore a big hat. He died when my children were little, so they didn't have all the beautiful experiences with him that I did. I knew him when there were no TVs, no modern gas heaters, so I got to sit on my grandfather's lap, beside the little fireplace in the corner, and listen to his stories. A lot of these beautiful things are gone nowadays, but both my husband and I try to fill these gaps by trying to share our experiences with our children."

Mary Trujillo
Cochiti

"Storytellers have a special meaning, I think, for past life when stories were a special thing for children, and the older people took more interest in the young. You were made to feel more important, to carry on for the future."

Dorothy Trujillo
Cochiti

"Stories were very important in our family. It was a way of passing down oral tradition, history, and language. Our storytellers were mainly, but not limited to, grandparents. Stories are told while stringing chili, sitting before a fireplace eating piñons, and so forth."

Frances Torivio Pino
Acoma

Plate 11. Dorothy Trujillo (Cochiti), Male Storyteller, 1980

After moving from her native Jemez to her husband's Pueblo, Dorothy became a major figurative artist, noted for her bold, crisp designs in both Storytellers and Nativities. In this large piece, one of the boys sitting on the Storyteller's boots holds a dog, and another has a drum; two other boys hold a football and large ball with a star pattern. Just barely visible here is the incised T-shape on the top of the adult's head, a distinctive feature in Dorothy's figures: "Some people ask me if that's my trademark — a 'T' for 'Trujillo' — but it's really to show the parting of the hair: the horizontal for the bangs, and the vertical for the center part."

Adobe Gallery, Albuquerque, New Mexico, 16 children, 11 inches high.

Plate 12. Frances Torivio Pino (Acoma), Female Storyteller, 1980

Frances began making pottery in the 1920s and Storytellers around 1968. The figure shown here reflects the long tradition of decorative pottery in her Pueblo. Since all six of the children are gathered on the front, the artist has decorated the back with pottery designs and modeled the entire figure in a jug shape. Minimal delineation of the neck, arms, legs, and feet emphasizes the rounded form. The open mouth and aquiline nose are modeled, while paint is reserved for the eyes, ceremonial rouge spots, and a rim of terra-cotta inside the mouth.

Adobe Gallery, Albuquerque, New Mexico, 6 children, 6½ inches high.

Plate 13. Ethel Shields (Acoma), Male Storyteller, 1983

Although this artist has also made more conventional Storytellers, in this figure she has used a pot to form the body of the Storyteller and has repeated the pottery designs on the cuffs of the adult's sleeves. All of Ethel's pot-shaped Storytellers are developed differently: they feature varying numbers of children and different pottery designs, and in some (like this one) entire legs are showing, while in others just the feet are visible.

Museum of Northern Arizona Gift Shop, Flagstaff, Arizona, 4 children, 10¼ inches high.

"I like doing large pots decorated with our Acoma motifs, so sometimes I work that into my Storytellers. In my days, storytellers were our TV and radio."

Ethel Shields
Acoma

"I made my first Storyteller when I moved back from California in 1973. A lot of people were asking me for them and they already had my sisters'. All my sisters encouraged me to make pottery, but my sister, Dorothy Trujillo, taught me how to shape and form Storytellers. I think these figures are popular because every potter who makes one has her own techniques in making them, and each Storyteller has its own facial expression. Grandparents were storytellers, but, as of today, the storyteller in our family is my dad, Louis Loretto. He still tells us the history of long ago."

Leonora (Lupe) Lucero
San Felipe

"After teaching clay classes at Jemez Day School for nine years, I had to stop in 1979 to keep up with my own pottery. I had so many orders to fill, and I wanted to try new things. Now it's nice when I go to shows and see my students winning prizes. Often they come up and thank me for starting them out."

Marie G. Romero
Jemez

Plate 14. Marilyn Henderson (Acoma), Female Storyteller, 1980

Marilyn Henderson began making bowls and animal figures when she was twelve years old, and in this female Storyteller she has combined her skills in both figurative work and in traditional pottery making. The adult figure holds an intricately patterned canteen, which becomes the focal point of the piece; the children hold three birds, a dog, and a drum; and the clothing of both the adult and children is lavishly decorated. Conversely, the artist's bowls, seed jars, wedding vases, and hunters' jugs always incorporate modeled figures.

Adobe Gallery, Albuquerque, New Mexico, 20 children, 10½ inches high.

Plate 15. Leonora (Lupe) Lucero (San Felipe), Male Storyteller, 1980

One of the six Loretto sisters from Jemez, Lupe later lived and worked in San Felipe. Her Storytellers are made from "Jemez clays and earth paints — white and gray for the slip, and red." Unlike the work of some of her sisters and most other Pueblo potters, her figures all have only two colors, a light, creamy buff and terra-cotta. Other distinctive characteristics are the nose, barely built out and forming a line with the cheekbones, the tiny mouth, the loop in the chongo knot, and the squash-blossom necklace that is modeled as well as painted.

Adobe Gallery, Albuquerque, New Mexico, 19 children, 8½ inches high.

Plate 16. Persingula M. Gachupin (Jemez), Female Storyteller, 1980

Long noted for her Jemez-style bowls and wedding vases, this artist was encouraged by her daughter, Marie G. Romero, to begin making Storytellers in the late 1960s. In this Storyteller, the adult has two distinctive features: well-delineated, wide-open eyes and a pursed mouth. Placement of the figure on a clay disc has become a characteristic of many Jemez figurative pieces.

Adobe Gallery, Albuquerque, New Mexico, 10 children, 7 inches high.

111

Plate 17. Marie G. Romero (Jemez), Female Storyteller, 1977

Marie Romero has focused her considerable skills on a wide variety of figurative subjects. In this classic version, the Storyteller is not placed on a disc, as are figures by many other Jemez artists; instead, the clay is extended out only in the front to form a footrest. All of the figures have modeled noses and painted eyes; the children's mouths are painted on, but the adult's is modeled and then outlined with a thin ring of terra-cotta. The back of the adult figure has a patterned terra-cotta sash and a matching band around her chongo knot.

Guy and Doris Monthan Collection, Flagstaff, Arizona, 6 children, 8 inches high.

Plate 18. Alma Concha Loretto (Jemez), Mudhead Storyteller, 1981

One of the six Loretto sisters, Alma returned to her native Jemez in the early 1980s, after living and working in Taos Pueblo for almost a dozen years. This figure is a unique interpretation of both the mudhead and the Storyteller — the adult is standing as he holds the five little mudheads. All wear feathers in their topknots, and painted detail is reserved for their boots and for the adult's manta and sash. Alma's Storytellers, Nativities, and most of her mudhead figures are done in just two colors — light buff and terra-cotta; the addition of black to this figure is a recent development.

Packard's Indian Trading Company, Santa Fe, New Mexico, 5 children, 8 inches high.

Plate 19. Mary E. Toya (Jemez), Female Storyteller, 1984

A well-known and prolific artist, Mary Toya has constantly set new challenges for herself. This figure is identified as "the world's largest Storyteller," and in terms of the number of children, it is. Most of the boys are lined up in columns on the right side, and the girls on the left. Among them, the children hold ten miniature pots (two are wedding vases suspended from strings), three baskets, two dogs, two balls, a drum, and two dolls (one of which is a miniature Storyteller, less than an inch high, with six babies). A long back apron, bordered with stepped terraces and a corn-stalk design with two butterflies, decorates the back of the figure.

Gilbert Ortega's Lincoln Village, Scottsdale, Arizona, 115 children, 18 inches high.

Plate 20. Carol Pecos (Jemez), Female Storyteller, 1983

This festive Storyteller is particularly complex and innovative. Thirty-one children cascade down the adult figure and ring the clay base on either side of her. On one side of the base are standing figures of a drummer with Indian headdress and a girl offering a platter of bread to two Eagle Dancers. On the other side (not visible) are a puppy with two young baseball players in team caps holding a ball, bat, and catcher's mitt, and a girl holding two babies, each of which holds a doll. Children placed on the figure are holding babies, puppies, a drum, a pot, a ball, and pieces of Indian bread with bites notched out of them. The back of the figure is decorated with a patterned apron and a yarn bow tied in the woman's chongo knot. The three-stranded necklace and earrings are made of tiny chunks of turquoise strung between white, red, and blue beads.

Clay Lockett Collection, Flagstaff, Arizona, 31 children, 12 inches high.

"When making my Storytellers and other potteries, I use Jemez clay and mineral paints made from rocks for the red, and wild spinach for the black. My husband, Casimiro, experimented with clay and rocks, looking for natural paints. My mother told me, 'If you find a rock and rub against it and get color off, this is the rock to use.' One day when the family was out on the mesa in Jemez hunting rabbits, my daughter, Henrietta, found just the right type of rock, which we have been using for the red color on our pottery ever since."

Mary E. Toya
Jemez

"When I was growing up, I remember this man who was an elder in the community, who was a very good storyteller. We used to go to this man's house and ask for stories. I remember especially the story about the 'Little-handed Coyote.' Today stories are still told in the family, but there aren't people like that anymore that everyone in the community goes to."

Carol Pecos
Jemez

"I come from a big family – six sisters and four brothers – and we hear stories every day about our lives. Everybody has a story to tell their children. My mom was Grace Loretto Fragua, and I think, deep in my heart, she's the one that taught my Storyteller. There's so many things she did for us; that all comes out in our Storytellers."

Emily Fragua Tsosie
Jemez

Plate 21. Emily Fragua Tsosie (Jemez), Koshare Clown Storyteller, 1980

A popular personage at Pueblo celebrations, the koshare clown is featured here in an unusual interpretation of the Storyteller. Like its ceremonial prototype, these clay koshares are painted in horizontal black and white stripes and have corn husks wrapped around the two traditional "horns" of hair. As in more conventional Storytellers by other Jemez artists, the figure is seated on a clay disc.

Adobe Gallery, Albuquerque, New Mexico, 2 children, 8½ inches high.

117

Plate 23. Alfred Aguilar (San Ildefonso), Hunter's Storyteller, 1982

In this interpretation, the eight children, dog, and buffalo are separated from the adult figure — a variation of the Storyteller theme which Helen Cordero called "The Children's Hour." The hunter wears a deerhide cape and holds a wooden bow and arrow; a gourd to carry water is slung over his shoulder.

Alfred Aguilar Indian Arts, San Ildefonso, New Mexico, 8 children, 7 inches high.

◀ **Plate 22. Manuel Vigil (Tesuque), Male Storyteller, 1981**

Manuel Vigil's Storytellers are unmistakable: the children are very large, and the figures are brightly painted. As is the custom in Tesuque pottery, this Storyteller was fashioned of native clay, then fired, and last painted with Bisque stain, a waterproof paint. Manuel, one of the most prolific figurative artists, did the modeling and sanding of this figure, while his wife, Vicenta, did the firing and painting. For fabric-clothed figures, Vicenta sews the clothes and accessories; here she has added rabbit-fur hair to the children.

Adobe Gallery, Albuquerque, New Mexico, 4 children, 5¼ inches high.

Plate 24. Maria I. Naranjo (Santa Clara), Female Storyteller, 1981

Maria Naranjo was the first Santa Clara potter to make Storytellers (1968). Most of her larger pieces have the quality of fine sculpture, as illustrated here, along with a favored technique of hers — the combining of matte surfaces and highly polished areas: in this figure the woman's polished redware dress and the children's beige and white clothes contrast with the matte finish of faces and hair. The gray hair is characteristic of many of Maria's polychrome figures; other trademarks are the texturing of the hair and the combination of modeled, incised, and painted facial features.

Adobe Gallery, Albuquerque, New Mexico, 4 children, 7 inches high.

Plate 25. Dorothy and Paul Gutierrez (Santa Clara), Mudhead Storyteller, 1980

In the figures of this husband-and-wife team, the modeling is done by Dorothy, and the sanding and polishing by Paul. They started doing miniature mudhead figures in 1976, and were among the first to depict them in Storyteller style. Three little mudheads were also included in one of their early blackware Nativity scenes. In this figure the adult and six babies are unpolished blackware, with high polish emphasizing the built-out areas of noses, eyes, ears, and topknots.

Adobe Gallery, Albuquerque, New Mexico, 6 children, 6¼ inches high.

"My great-grandfather used to tell us fairy tales, like the coyote story and rabbit stories. The one I remember is 'The Giant from Black Mesa.' He told us when kids are bad, the giant will come down and put them in gunnysacks, and take them up to Black Mesa and put them in the ovens. There are two humps on the side of the Mesa that look like our outdoor ovens or hornos, *as we call them, so it seemed very real to us, something that could happen. The Hunter (Pl. 23) is telling of his hunt; the buffalo in the scene is symbolic, the one he tried to shoot. I wanted to do something different, and I thought of how when we go hunting, we come home and tell of the experiences we had."*

Alfred Aguilar
("Sä Wä Pin")
San Ildefonso

"I decided to make Storytellers because it was a chance to express many faces on many figures. No one needed to encourage me; they were just fun to make. I started with a bear Storyteller with cubs, and from there just adding more – frog, raccoon, and other animal or clown Storytellers."

Margaret Gutierrez
Santa Clara

"I have noted that a lot of the people who buy my figures are librarians, teachers, and grandmothers; they seem to make an association between the storytellers and themselves. When doing the faces of my figures, I never put a nose on them, because that gives them too much character. Grand-mother is thinking about the story she's telling; that's why her eyes are closed."

Stella Teller
Isleta

Plate 26. Margaret and Luther Gutierrez (Santa Clara), Koshare Clown Storyteller, 1981

Internationally known simply by their first names, this sister-and-brother team began working together in 1966. The modeling of their figures is done by Margaret and the painted decoration by Luther. In this whimsical version of the Storyteller, three mudhead clowns are added to the koshares, making a total of twelve children. The corn husks traditionally wrapped around the koshare clown's hair "horns" are represented by tufts of straw. The artists' trademarks — animated expressions and highly polished surfaces — are clearly evident here, along with their typical colors — buff clay with detailing of black, white, terra-cotta, and small touches of gray.

Adobe Gallery, Albuquerque, New Mexico, 12 children, 4½ inches high.

Plate 27. Stella Teller (Isleta), Navajo Storyteller, 1981

Stella Teller was the first artist to produce the Navajo-style Storyteller and the first to use gray extensively. Her figures also feature more white than those of most potters; only the faces here are beige. To achieve her subtle coloring she has used white and red clay, and for the gray, mixed white with manganese. Another of Stella's innovations was to incorporate turquoise stones in her figures; here they are set into the Navajo woman's concho belt and necklace. The patterned skirt flares out to become an important part of the design and serves as a stable base for the figure.

Adobe Gallery, Albuquerque, New Mexico, 11 children, 7½ inches high.

PART III

Pueblo Storyteller Potters

Biographical Survey of the Artists

The following survey documents information on 110 artists who made Storytellers or related figures between the mid-1960s and mid-1980s. In the column that records when individual potters began making Storytellers, the date given sometimes precedes the advent of the Storyteller as conceived by Helen Cordero in 1964. In some of these cases, the artists were referring to Singing Mothers or to Mother and Child figurines, which they later called Storytellers. In other cases, the earlier date refers to animal or bird figures with babies on them, such as the composite owls made in Acoma and Zuni, which collectors and others (although not necessarily the artists) referred to as Storyteller Owls after the Storyteller theme became popular. In the case of Lorencita Pino, of Tesuque, the 1955 date refers to the year that she began placing small figures on her Rain God figurines.

The names of 189 other potters in the artists' families also appear in this survey; at least 50 of them are known to have made Storytellers or other figures related to this tradition. The list at the end of the survey includes these 50 family members (indicated by asterisks) along with 80 additional figurative artists whom we were unable to locate.

The artists' names are given in alphabetical order under their Pueblos, which are listed by language group in the order that they appear in the text of Part I — i.e., Keres Pueblos, the Towa Pueblo of Jemez, Tewa Pueblos, Tiwa Pueblos, and Zuni Pueblo.

Name of Artist	Date of Birth	Date of First Storyteller	Person Who Taught Artist Pottery Making	Potters in the Artist's Family
COCHITI				
Josephine Arquero	12-31-28	ca. 1969	*Mother:* Damacia Cordero	*Sisters:* Martha Arquero Gloria Arquero Marie Lewake
Martha Arquero	5-15-45	ca. 1975	*Mother:* Damacia Cordero	*Sisters:* Josephine Arquero Gloria Arquero Marie Lewake
Buffy Cordero	11-28-69	ca. 1980	*Grandmother:* Helen Cordero *Teacher at school*	*Father:* George Cordero *Cousins:* Tim Cordero Kevin Peshlakai *Aunt:* Antonita Suina
Damacia Cordero	12-1905	ca. 1920	*Mother:* Lucinda Suina	*Daughters:* Josephine Arquero Martha Arquero Gloria Arquero Marie Lewake
George Cordero	9-24-44	1982	*Mother:* Helen Cordero	*Daughter:* Buffy Cordero *Nephews:* Tim Cordero Kevin Peshlakai *Sister:* Antonita Suina
Helen Cordero	6-17-15	1964	*Cousin-in-law:* Juanita Arquero	*Son:* George Cordero *Daughter:* Antonita Suina *Grandsons:* Tim Cordero Kevin Peshlakai *Granddaughters:* Buffy Cordero Evon Trujillo *Daughters-in-law:* Kathy Trujillo Mary T. Trujillo

Name of Artist	Date of Birth	Date of First Storyteller	Person Who Taught Artist Pottery Making	Potters in the Artist's Family
Tim Cordero	8-25-63	1980	*Grandmother:* Helen Cordero	*Uncle:* George Cordero *Aunt:* Antonita Suina *Cousins:* Buffy Cordero Kevin Peshlakai
Tony Dallas	3-23-56	1982	*Mother-in-law:* Lucy R. Suina	*None*
Ivan and Rita Lewis (husband and wife)	Ivan, 8-24-19 Rita, 1-7-20	ca. 1973 ca. 1973	*Self-taught by observing mother:* Lucy Lewis *Self-taught by observing mother:* Ascencion Banada	*Ivan's sisters:* Doris Lewis Emma Lewis *Rita's aunt:* Ignacita Arquero *Ivan and Rita's daughter:* Patricia Lewis *Daughter-in-law:* Mary Lewis
Mary Martin	6-17-27	ca. 1974	*Friend:* Dorothy Trujillo	*Grandmother:* Seferina Suina *Cousins:* Seferina Ortiz Ada Suina *Daughters:* Gladys Martin Adrienne Martin

"When firing, the weather must be calm; if it is windy, figurines become smoked, which may result in a second firing. Firing depends on mother nature. It involves big chance and prayer."

Mary Martin
Cochiti

Name of Artist	Date of Birth	Date of First Storyteller	Person Who Taught Artist Pottery Making	Potters in the Artist's Family
Louis and Virginia A. Naranjo (husband and wife)	Louis, 8-17-32	ca. 1974	*Self-taught by observing mother:* Frances Suina	*Louis's sister:* Sarah Suina *Virginia's aunt:* Juanita Arquero *Virginia's cousin:* Ada Suina
	Virginia, 10-19-32	ca. 1974	*Self-taught by observing mother-in-law:* Frances Suina	
Seferina Ortiz	10-1-31	ca. 1962	*Mother:* Laurencita Herrera	*Grandmothers:* Reyes Romero Seferina Suina *Great-aunt:* Estephanita Herrera *Children:* Joyce Ortiz Lewis Janice Oritz Juanita I. Ortiz Virgil Ortiz
Kevin Peshlakai	9-64	ca. 1981	*Grandmother:* Helen Cordero	*Uncle:* George Cordero *Aunt:* Antonita Suina *Cousins:* Buffy Cordero Tim Cordero
Stephanie C. Rhoades ("Snow Flake Flower")	12-26-32	ca. 1979	*Partially self-taught, with some help from* Mary Martin	*Grandmother:* Estephanita Herrera *Sister:* Ada Suina *Children:* Jonathan Loretto Morningstar Rhoades
Maria Priscilla Romero	9-12-36	1979	*Mother:* Maggie Chalan *Mother-in-law:* Teresita Romero	*Daughter:* Mary Eunice Ware

Name of Artist	Date of Birth	Date of First Storyteller	Person Who Taught Artist Pottery Making	Potters in the Artist's Family
Ada Suina	5-30-30	1976	*Cousin:* Virginia Naranjo *Mother-in-law:* Aurelia Suina	*Grandmother:* Estephanita Herrera *Sister:* Stephanie Rhoades *Children:* Caroline Grace Suina Marie Charlotte Suina Maria Suina Patty Suina
Antonita (Tony) Suina	6-7-48	1983	*Mother:* Helen Cordero	*Brother:* George Cordero *Niece:* Buffy Cordero *Nephews:* Tim Cordero Kevin Peshlakai
Aurelia Suina	10-30-11	ca. 1968	*Mother:* Victoria Montoya *Aunt:* Reycita Romero	*Daughter-in-law:* Ada Suina *Granddaughters:* Caroline Grace Suina Marie Charlotte Suina Maria Suina Patty Suina
Caroline Grace Suina	11-7-55	ca. 1980	*Mother:* Ada Suina	*Grandmother:* Aurelia Suina *Sisters:* Marie Charlotte Suina Maria Suina Patty Suina
Frances Suina	9-2-02	ca. 1965	———	*Son:* Louis Naranjo *Daughter-in-law:* Virginia A. Naranjo *Daughter:* Sarah Suina

Name of Artist	Date of Birth	Date of First Storyteller	Person Who Taught Artist Pottery Making	Potters in the Artist's Family
Judith Suina	4-14-60	1978	*Mother:* Dorothy Trujillo	*Sisters:* Frances Pino Cecilia Valencia *Brother:* Onofre Trujillo II *Mother-in-law:* Louise Q. Suina *Sister-in-law:* Vangie Suina *Aunt and great-aunts:* (*see* Dorothy Trujillo)
Louise Q. Suina	10-2-39	1979	*Mostly self-taught, with some help from cousin:* Dorothy Trujillo	*Daughter:* Vangie Suina *Cousins:* Helen Cordero Seferina Ortiz *Daughter-in-law:* Judith Suina
Lucy R. Suina	3-9-21	ca. 1974	*Mother:* Reyes T. Romero *Father:* Vicente Romero	*Sister:* Laurencita Herrera *Niece:* Seferina Ortiz *Cousin:* Helen Cordero *Daughter:* Evangeline Suina
Marie Charlotte Suina	7-19-54	ca. 1980	*Mother:* Ada Suina	*Grandmother:* Aurelia Suina *Cousins:* Josephine Arquero Martha Arquero *Sisters:* Caroline Grace Suina Maria Suina Patty Suina
Vangie Suina	4-25-59	1981	*Mother:* Louise Q. Suina	*Grandmother:* Anita Suina *Great-aunt:* Marianita Venado

Name of Artist	Date of Birth	Date of First Storyteller	Person Who Taught Artist Pottery Making	Potters in the Artist's Family
Del Trancosa	8-2-51	1980	*Mother-in-law:* Helen Cordero	*None*
Dorothy Trujillo	4-26-32	1966	*Mother:* Carrie Reid Loretto *Grandmother:* Lupe Madalena Loretto	*Aunts:* Loretta Cajero Damacia Cordero *(through marriage)* *Sisters:* Marie Edna Coriz Alma Concha Loretto Fannie Wall Loretto Leonora (Lupe) Lucero Mary E. Toya *Daughters:* Frances Pino Judith Suina Cecilia Valencia *Son:* Onofre Trujillo II

"*Helen Cordero and I are first cousins and had the same grandfather, Santiago Quintana, who used to tell all of us grandchildren so many good stories. We lived with him, and my mother, Reyes T. Romero, took care of him. The predictions he made all have come true, like the big Cochiti Dam we have now. Way back in the 1930s he told us, 'The White Man will change the course of our rivers.' Then, when my cousin, Ben Quintana, and another boy cousin were about ten, they were looking up at the stars one night and asked my grandfather about the future. He said, 'Look at the sky first for the parrot messengers.' One star had a very bad message. Our grandfather looked sad, and he said, 'By the time you two boys are of age, there will be a war, and you will go to the far corners of the earth.' Whenever we asked about it later, he always looked sad. 'He'll never come back,' he said. My cousin Ben served in World War II and was sent to the Philippines. He did not come back.*"

Lucy R. Suina
Cochiti

Name of Artist	Date of Birth	Date of First Storyteller	Person Who Taught Artist Pottery Making	Potters in the Artist's Family
Evon Trujillo	1-2-59	ca. 1980	*Mother:* Kathy Trujillo	*Grandmothers:* Rosalie Aguilar Helen Cordero *Grandfather:* Jose A. Aguilar *Aunts:* Florence A. Naranjo Annie A. Martinez *Uncles:* Alfred Aguilar Jose V. Aguilar, Sr. *Cousin:* Becky Martinez
Felipa Trujillo	4-27-08	ca. 1965	*Mother:* Estephanita Herrera	*Daughter:* Angel Quintana *Niece (through marriage):* Helen Cordero
Kathy Trujillo	8-28-31	ca. 1980	*Mother:* Rosalie Aguilar *Father:* Jose A. Aguilar *For Storytellers:* Dorothy Trujillo and Mary Martin	*Daughter:* Evon Trujillo *Sisters:* Florence A. Naranjo Annie A. Martinez *Brothers:* Alfred Aguilar Jose V. Aguilar, Sr. *Niece:* Becky Martinez *Mother-in-law:* Helen Cordero
Mary T. Trujillo	5-26-37	ca. 1980	*Mother:* Leonidas C. Tapia *For Storytellers, Mother-in-law:* Helen Cordero *Neighbor:* Ada Suina	*Aunts:* Belen Tapia Santianita Suazo Martina Aquino *Great-aunt:* Rose Gonzales *Brother:* Tom Tapia *Cousins:* Anita Suazo Tse-Pe

Name of Artist	Date of Birth	Date of First Storyteller	Person Who Taught Artist Pottery Making	Potters in the Artist's Family
Onofre Trujillo II	6-15-69	1982	*Mother:* Dorothy Trujillo	*Sisters:* Frances Pino Judith Suina Cecilia Valencia *Aunts and great-aunts:* (*see* Dorothy Trujillo)
Mary Eunice Ware	10-4-58	ca. 1980	*Mother:* Maria Priscilla Romero	*Grandmother:* Teresita Romero *Great-grandmother:* Cresencia Quintana

ACOMA

Name of Artist	Date of Birth	Date of First Storyteller	Person Who Taught Artist Pottery Making	Potters in the Artist's Family
Blanche Antonio	5-10-27	ca. 1978	*Mother:* Juana Pasqual *Grandmother:* Juana Concho	*Clan Grandmother:* Marie Z. Chino *Sister:* Mary Lukee *Sister-in-law:* Romolda Pasqual *Nieces:* Bonnie Leno Kimberly Pasqual
Hilda Antonio	8-7-38	ca. 1958	*Mother:* Eva B. Histia	*Grandmother:* Helice Valdo *Daughter:* Mary A. Garcia *Sister:* Rose Torivio *Aunts:* Lucy Lewis Elizabeth Woncada
Wanda Aragon	11-21-48	ca. 1972	*Mother:* Frances Torivio Pino	*Sister:* Lillian Salvador *Mother-in-law:* Daisy Aragon *Sister-in-law:* Rose Torivio *Aunts:* (*see* Frances Torivio Pino)

> *"My paternal grandmother, Juanalita Histia, was the storyteller I remember best. When she came to our house, she would call all the little children to gather around her, and call out to my mother: 'Time to roast the piñons!' My mother would set the roasted piñons and parched corn in the middle of the floor, with the children sitting around it. We would eat in order to keep awake. Then my grandmother would tell us stories about a long time ago, how she grew up, how our ancestors made pottery, and how, during the wars, the people of Acoma hired the owls to watch over the Pueblo at night."*
>
> **Hilda Antonio**
> **Acoma**

Name of Artist	Date of Birth	Date of First Storyteller	Person Who Taught Artist Pottery Making	Potters in the Artist's Family
Joyce Leno Barreras	10-17-55	1980	*Mother:* Juana Leno	*Sisters:* Rose Leno Chavez Mary J. Leno Phyllis Leno Regina M. Leno Shutiva
Rose Leno Chavez	11-18-43	1982	*Mother:* Juana Leno	*Sisters:* Joyce Leno Barreras Mary J. Leno Phyllis Leno Regina M. Leno Shutiva
Marilyn Henderson	8-14-54	1978	*Grandmother:* Dolores Sanchez	*Sisters:* Carolyn Concho Diane Lewis Sharon Lewis Rebecca Lucario
Linda Juanico	9-1-27	1972	*Grandmother:* Teofila Torivio	*Daughter:* Carmen King *Mother:* Mamie Ortiz *Sisters:* Rachael Arnold Myrna Chino *Aunts and cousins:* (*see* Frances Torivio Pino)

Name of Artist	Date of Birth	Date of First Storyteller	Person Who Taught Artist Pottery Making	Potters in the Artist's Family
Juana Leno	3-4-17	ca. 1976	*Mother:* Lupita Vallo *Grandmother:* Eulilia Vallo	*Daughters:* Joyce Leno Barreras Rose Leno Chavez Mary J. Leno Phyllis Leno Regina M. Leno Shutiva
Mary Lowden	12-24-41	1980	*Self-taught*	*Grandmother-in-law:* Lupe Chavez *Sister-in-law:* Virginia Lowden
Mary Lukee	8-17-32	ca. 1978	*Mother:* Juana Pasqual	*Sister:* Blanche Antonio *Sister-in-law and nieces:* (*see* Juana Pasqual)
Juana Pasqual	1-17-1900	ca. 1978	*Mother:* Juana Concho	*Daughters:* Blanche Antonio Mary Lukee *Daughter-in-law:* Romolda Pasqual *Granddaughters:* Bonnie Leno Kimberly Pasqual

"*When I was twenty years old, I found a shard that was made like a figurine, and I decided to make one like the one I found. Storytellers must have been important, since that small figure I found dated back in time. When I make them now, I use native clay and paint from wild spinach and mineral rocks. I mold the clay with my hands — shaping, putting arms and legs on — using hands only, no tools. This is the only kind of pottery I work with, and I rely solely on touch, for I am totally blind.*"

**Linda Juanico
Acoma**

Name of Artist	Date of Birth	Date of First Storyteller	Person Who Taught Artist Pottery Making	Potters in the Artist's Family
Frances Torivio Pino	4-1-05	ca. 1968	*Self-taught by observing mother:* Teofila Torivio	*Daughters:* Wanda Aragon Ruth Paisano Lucy Reed Lillian Salvador Sandra Scisson *Sisters:* Katherine Analla Lolita Concho Conception Garcia Juanita Keene Mamie Ortiz
Lillian Salvador	4-6-44	ca. 1976	*Mother:* Frances Torivio Pino	*Sister:* Wanda Aragon *Other sisters and aunts:* (see Frances Torivio Pino)
Ethel Shields	9-17-26	ca. 1976	*Mother:* Dolores Sanchez	*Daughter:* Charmae Natseway *Son:* Jack Shields
Jack Shields	8-22-61	ca. 1978	*Mother:* Ethel Shields	*Sister:* Charmae Natseway
Rose Torivio	5-14-35	ca. 1973	*Mother:* Eva B. Histia	*Sister:* Hilda Antonio *Aunts:* Lucy Lewis Elizabeth Woncada

SANTO DOMINGO

Marie Edna Coriz	2-3-46	ca. 1978	*Mother:* Carrie R. Loretto *For Storytellers, Sister:* Dorothy Trujillo	*Daughter:* Angel Annette Coriz *Sisters:* Alma Concha Loretto Fannie Wall Loretto

Name of Artist	Date of Birth	Date of First Storyteller	Person Who Taught Artist Pottery Making	Potters in the Artist's Family
Marie Edna Coriz (*cont.*)				Leonora (Lupe) Lucero Mary E. Toya *Nieces and nephews:* (*see* sisters' children)

SAN FELIPE

Name of Artist	Date of Birth	Date of First Storyteller	Person Who Taught Artist Pottery Making	Potters in the Artist's Family
Lenora (Lupe) Lucero	12-6-43	1973	*Mother:* Carrie R. Loretto *For Storytellers, Sister:* Dorothy Trujillo	*Sisters:* Marie Edna Coriz Alma Concha Loretto Fannie Wall Loretto Mary E. Toya *Children:* Xavier S. Lucero Felicia M. Lucero *Nieces and nephews:* (*see* sisters' children)
Cecilia Valencia	10-12-54	ca. 1973	*Mother:* Dorothy Trujillo	*Brother:* Onofre Trujillo II *Sisters:* Frances Pino Judith Suina *Aunts:* Marie Edna Coriz Alma Concha Loretto Fannie Wall Loretto Leonora (Lupe) Lucero Mary E. Toya *Cousins:* (*see* children of above)

Name of Artist	Date of Birth	Date of First Storyteller	Person Who Taught Artist Pottery Making	Potters in the Artist's Family
ZIA				
Adrienne Shije	3-23-56	1980	*For Storytellers,* Alma Concha Loretto Marie G. Romero *For Pottery, Mother-in-law:* Eusebia Shije	*Grandmother:* Marie Toledo *Godmother:* Dorothy Trujillo *Daughter:* Marie Shije

The Towa Pueblo of Jemez

Loretta Cajero	4-4-16	ca. 1979	*Mother:* Lupe Madalena Loretto	*Daughter:* Frances Casiquito *Grandson:* Gabriel Casiquito Cajero *Nieces:* Marie Edna Coriz Alma Concha Loretto Fannie Wall Loretto Leonora Lupe Lucero Mary E. Toya Dorothy Trujillo
Edwina (Bonnie) Fragua	3-24-66	1978	*Mother:* Grace Fragua *Sister:* Emily Tsosie *Teacher in 5th grade:* Marie G. Romero	*Grandmother:* Emilia Loretto *Sisters:* Cindy Fragua Felicia Fragua Rose Fragua Carol F. Gachupin
Felicia Fragua	10-23-64	1981	*Mother:* Grace Fragua *Sister:* Edwina (Bonnie) Fragua	*Grandmother:* Emilia Loretto *Sisters:* Cindy Fragua Rose Fragua Carol F. Gachupin Emily Tsosie

Name of Artist	Date of Birth	Date of First Storyteller	Person Who Taught Artist Pottery Making	Potters in the Artist's Family
Lenora G. Fragua	4-18-38	ca. 1975	*Self-taught*	*Mother:* Persingula Gachupin *Sister:* Marie G. Romero *Daughters:* Virginia Fragua Bertha Gachupin *Nieces:* Laura Gachupin Maxine Toya *Cousin:* Juanita Fragua
Melinda Toya Fragua	3-18-59	1978	*Mother:* Mary E. Toya	*Sisters:* Henrietta Gachupin Anita Toya Judith Toya Marie Roberta Toya Mary Ellen Toya Yolanda Toya *Aunts:* Marie Edna Coriz Alma Concha Loretto Fannie Wall Loretto Leonora (Lupe) Lucero Dorothy Trujillo
Rose T. Fragua	5-7-46	ca. 1979	*Mother:* Grace Fragua *Sister:* Emily Tsosie	*Grandmother:* Emilia Loretto *Sisters:* Cindy Fragua Edwina (Bonnie) Fragua Felicia Fragua Carol F. Gachupin *Daughter:* Janeth Fragua *Cousins:* Caroline Loretto Geraldine Sandia

Name of Artist	Date of Birth	Date of First Storyteller	Person Who Taught Artist Pottery Making	Potters in the Artist's Family
Caroline Fragua Gachupin ✓	7-12-53	1974	*Mother:* Grace Fragua *Sister:* Emily Tsosie	*Husband:* Joseph R. Gachupin *Sisters:* Edwina (Bonnie) Fragua Cindy Fragua ✓ Felicia Fragua Rose Fragua *Brothers:* Phillip Fragua Clifford Fragua Ben Fragua *Niece:* Janeth Fragua *Nephew:* Joseph L. Fragua *Cousins:* Caroline Loretto Geraldine Sandia
Henrietta Toya Gachupin	1-20-63	1982	*Mother:* Mary E. Toya	*Mother-in-law:* Alice Gachupin *Sisters:* Melinda Toya Fragua Anita Toya Judith Toya Marie Roberta Toya Mary Ellen Toya Yolanda Toya *Aunts:* (*see* Melinda Toya Fragua)
Laura Gachupin	11-4-54	1983	*Self-taught by observing mother:* Marie G. Romero *and sister:* Maxine R. Toya	*Son:* Gordon Foley *Grandmother:* Persingula Gachupin *Aunt:* Lenora Fragua *Great-aunt:* Lupe Romero

Name of Artist	Date of Birth	Date of First Storyteller	Person Who Taught Artist Pottery Making	Potters in the Artist's Family
Persingula M. Gachupin	1910	ca. 1968	*Self-taught*	*Sister:* Lupe Romero *Daughters:* Lenora Fragua Marie G. Romero *Granddaughters:* Virginia Fragua Bertha Gachupin Laura Gachupin Maxine Toya
Alma Concha ✓ Loretto	10-9-41	1969	*Mother:* Carrie Reid Loretto *Aunt:* Loretta Cajero	*Children:* Antoinette Concha Delfino Concha, Jr. John Concha Justin Concha Monica Concha Renee Concha Vernon Concha *Sisters:* Marie Edna Coriz Fannie Wall Loretto Leonora (Lupe) Lucero Mary E. Toya Dorothy Trujillo *Grandmother:* Lupe Madalena Loretto *Cousin:* Carol Pecos
Debbie Loretto	4-16-56	1982	*Mother:* Caroline Seonia	*Brother:* Kenneth Seonia, Jr. *Sister-in-law:* Santana Seonia *Son:* Florentino Loretto
Estella Loretto	1-26-54	ca. 1980	*Mother:* Albenita Loretto	*Sister:* Rose DeVore

Name of Artist	Date of Birth	Date of First Storyteller	Person Who Taught Artist Pottery Making	Potters in the Artist's Family
Fannie Wall Loretto	4-22-50	ca. 1978	*Sisters:* Marie Edna Coriz Alma Concha Loretto Leonora (Lupe) Lucero Mary E. Toya Dorothy Trujillo	*Mother:* Carrie Reid Loretto *Grandmother:* Lupe Madalena Loretto *Daughter:* Kathleen Wall *Aunt:* Loretta Cajero *Cousin:* Carol Pecos
Frances Yepa Montoya	4-4-56	1971	*Mother:* Marie G. Yepa *Teacher at Jemez Day School:* Marie G. Romero	*Sister:* Florinda Yepa
Carol Pecos	5-1-34	ca. 1974	*Mother:* Louisa F. Toledo	*Daughters:* Jackie Pecos Rose Pecos— Sun Rhodes Stephanie Pecos *Son:* Irwin Louis Pecos *Daughter-in-law:* Jeannette Pecos *Grandmother:* Lupe Madalena Loretto *Aunt:* Loretta Cajero *Cousins:* Marie Edna Coriz Alma Concha Loretto Fannie Wall Loretto Leonora (Lupe) Lucero Mary E. Toya Dorothy Trujillo

Name of Artist	Date of Birth	Date of First Storyteller	Person Who Taught Artist Pottery Making	Potters in the Artist's Family
Jeannette Pecos	8-30-53	ca. 1979	*Mother-in-law:* Carol Pecos	*Husband:* Irwin Louis Pecos *Sisters-in-law:* Jackie Pecos Rose Pecos— Sun Rhodes Stephanie Pecos
Rose Pecos— Sun Rhodes	5-23-56	ca. 1979	*Grandmother:* Louisa F. Toledo *Mother:* Carol Pecos	*Brother:* Irwin Louis Pecos *Sisters:* Jackie Pecos Stephanie Pecos *Sister-in-law:* Jeannette Pecos
Lupe Romero	11-14-02	ca. 1978	*Mother:* Benina Madina Madalena	*Daughter:* Persingula Tosa *Granddaughters:* Lorencita Madalena Mary Madalena Dorale Tosa Antonita Toya *Niece:* Marie G. Romero
Marie G. Romero	7-27-27	ca. 1968	*Self-taught by observing mother:* Persingula M. Gachupin	*Daughters:* Laura Gachupin Maxine Toya *Sister:* Lenora Fragua *Grandmother:* Benina Madina Madalena *Aunt:* Lupe Romero *Nieces:* Virginia Fragua Bertha Gachupin *Cousins:* Juanita Fragua Persingula Tosa

Name of Artist	Date of Birth	Date of First Storyteller	Person Who Taught Artist Pottery Making	Potters in the Artist's Family
Caroline Seonia	3-30-28	ca. 1978	*Self-taught by observing mother:* Persingula Loretto	*Daughter:* Debbie Loretto *Son:* Kenneth Seonia, Jr. *Daughter-in-law:* Santana Seonia
Santana Seonia	7-21-48	1982	*Mother:* Juanita T. Toledo	*Mother-in-law:* Caroline Seonia *Sister-in-law:* Debbie Loretto *Sister:* Margaret Toledo *Aunt:* Amlita Toledo *Cousin:* Juanita Martinez
Persingula Tosa	7-9-24	ca. 1972	*Mother:* Lupe Romero	*Daughters:* Mary Madalena Dorale Tosa

"My grandfather told many stories that his grandfather told him, but he died when I was born, so my father and mother were the storytellers then. We would sit in front of the fire on a bear rug or a goatskin or sheepskin as they told stories that were passed down from my great-great-grandfather and some way before then. Many of the stories were things for little children that were like fairy tales and nursery rhymes, but some were telling the future. My great-grandfather and other old-timers said of coming generations: 'An iron bird will fly them, and air will carry them, and there will be iron roads to carry them.' So there they were, telling of airplanes and balloons and railroads. . . . How did they know way back then? Another thing I remember hearing about the old-timers: they were against tractors going into the fields; they wanted only the old, homemade, wood plows to be used, no iron plows. They did not think it was right to leave machine tracks in the earth, just people tracks."

**Caroline Seonia
Jemez**

Name of Artist	Date of Birth	Date of First Storyteller	Person Who Taught Artist Pottery Making	Potters in the Artist's Family

Anita Toya	8-24-60	1981	*Mother:*
			Mary E. Toya
				Sisters:
				Melinda Fragua
				Henrietta Gachupin
				Judith Toya
				Marie Roberta Toya
				Mary Ellen Toya
				Yolanda Toya
				Aunts:
				Marie Edna Coriz
				Alma Concha
				  Loretto
				Fannie Wall Loretto
				Leonora (Lupe)
				  Lucero
				Dorothy Trujillo

Judith Toya ✓	9-19-54	1981	*Mother:* Mary E. Toya	*Sisters:* Melinda Fragua Henrietta Gachupin Anita Toya Marie Roberta Toya Mary Ellen Toya Yolanda Toya *Aunts:* (*see* Anita Toya)
Marie Roberta Toya	7-6-56	1980	*Mother:* Mary E. Toya	*Sisters:* Melinda Fragua Henrietta Gachupin Anita Toya Judith Toya Mary Ellen Toya Yolanda Toya *Aunts:* (*see* Anita Toya)

Mary E. Toya	5-29-34	ca. 1973	*Mother:*
			Carrie Reid
			  Loretto
			Grandmother:
			Lupe Madalena
			  Loretto
				Sisters:
				Marie Edna Coriz
				Alma Concha
				  Loretto
				Fannie Wall Loretto
				Leonora (Lupe)
				  Lucero
				Dorothy Trujillo
				Daughters:
				Melinda Fragua

Name of Artist	Date of Birth	Date of First Storyteller	Person Who Taught Artist Pottery Making	Potters in the Artist's Family
Mary E. Toya (*cont.*)				Henrietta Gachupin Anita Toya Judith Toya Marie Roberta Toya Mary Ellen Toya Yolanda Toya *Aunt:* Loretta Cajero
Mary Ellen Toya	3-28-55	ca. 1979	*Mother:* Mary E. Toya	*Sisters:* Melinda Fragua Henrietta Gachupin Anita Toya Judith Toya Marie Roberta Toya Yolanda Toya *Aunts:* (*see* Anita Toya)
Maxine R. Toya	4-25-48	ca. 1980	*Mother:* Marie G. Romero	*Sister:* Laura Gachupin *Son:* Damian Toya *Daughter:* Camilla Toya *Grandmother:* Persingula Gachupin

"*My husband Casimiro's family were among the seventeen survivors from Pecos who came to settle here, and his grandmother and grandfather had many stories to tell of those times. They were the storytellers that I remember in our family. Long ago I think men were the traditional storytellers. Lately women are shown in that role, and I think that's for fertility reasons. I think that's why they are so popular. Some of my customers order Storyteller figures according to how many children they themselves have. If they have five children, then they want a Storyteller with five children on it, too.*"

Mary E. Toya
Jemez

Name of Artist	Date of Birth	Date of First Storyteller	Person Who Taught Artist Pottery Making	Potters in the Artist's Family
Maxine R. Toya (*cont.*)				*Aunt:* Lenora Fragua *Great-aunt:* Lupe Romero
Yolanda Toya	4-20-67	1983	*Mother:* Mary E. Toya	*Sisters:* Melinda Fragua Henrietta Gachupin Anita Toya Judith Toya Marie Roberta Toya Mary Ellen Toya *Aunts:* (*see* Anita Toya)
Emily Fragua Tsosie	6-4-51	ca. 1973	*Self-taught by observing mother:* Grace Fragua	*Sisters:* Cindy Fragua Edwina (Bonnie) Fragua Felicia Fragua Rose T. Fragua Carol F. Gachupin *Cousins:* Marie Edna Coriz Caroline Loretto Alma Concha Loretto Fannie Wall Loretto Leonora (Lupe) Lucero Geraldine Sandia Mary E. Toya Dorothy Trujillo
Florinda Yepa	9-25-54	1981	*Mother:* Marie G. Yepa *Sister:* Frances Yepa Montoya	*Sons:* Emmett Yepa Manuel Yepa

Tewa Pueblos

Name of Artist	Date of Birth	Date of First Storyteller	Person Who Taught Artist Pottery Making	Potters in the Artist's Family
TESUQUE				
Lorencita Pino	9-23-1900	ca. 1955	*Mother:* Myphia Herrera	*Daughter:* Eva Mitchell *Son:* Joseph B. Pino *Sister-in-law:* Anastasia Pino *Grandmother:* "Sunflower"
Manuel Vigil	6-10-1900	ca. 1977	*Mother:* Anastasia Vigil	*Wife:* Vicenta Vigil *Daughters:* Anna Marie Lovato Eliza Ruth Vigil *Grandson:* Art Vigil
NAMBE				
Marie Priscilla Herrera	12-18-43	1978	*Self-taught*	*Great-grandmother:* Perfilia Pena *Great-aunt:* Josefita Anaya *Aunt:* Domatilla Perez

"My mother's Rain Gods were white, made of our natural clay, with black painted on them. For her black paint she boils wild spinach and makes a gel of it which she can save for future use. She makes some of her Storyteller figures in our micaceous clay which are left unpainted, and others of our regular clay which are painted with acrylics. Years ago we used to use poster paints, but they wash off, so now we use acrylics."

**Eva Mitchell,
daughter of Lorencita Pino
Tesuque**

Name of Artist	Date of Birth	Date of First Storyteller	Person Who Taught Artist Pottery Making	Potters in the Artist's Family
Marie Priscilla Herrera (*cont.*)				*Sisters:* Virginia Gutierrez Emiliana Gadd Vigil *Cousin:* Lonie Vigil
Emiliana Gadd Vigil	9-17-42	ca. 1972	*Self-taught*	*Great-grandmother:* Perfilia Pena *Great-aunt:* Josefita Anaya *Aunt:* Domatilla Perez *Sisters:* Marie P. Herrera Virginia Gutierrez *Cousin:* Lonie Vigil

SAN JUAN

Reycita Garcia	1-4-31	ca. 1955	*Mother:* Geronima Archulata	*Aunt:* Gregorita Trujillo *Son:* Gordon Garcia

SAN ILDEFONSO

Alfred Aguilar ("Sä Wä Pin")	7-1-33	ca. 1975	*Self-taught*	*Mother:* Rosalie Aguilar *Father:* Jose A. Aguilar *Sisters:* Annie A. Martinez Florence A. Naranjo Kathy Trujillo *Brother:* Jose V. Aguilar, Sr.

> *"All of my Storytellers are made in polished blackware and are seated on drums made of driftwood. All of them are elderly men talking to young boys. I believe the men were the storytellers, because when I was young, we used to sit and listen to them during any dance or before or after any meeting. They would tell jokes or talk about the past, which sometimes was scary."*
>
> **Jose V. Aguilar, Sr.**
> **("Yellowbird")**
> **San Ildefonso**

Name of Artist	Date of Birth	Date of First Storyteller	Person Who Taught Artist Pottery Making	Potters in the Artist's Family
Jose V. Aguilar, Sr. ("Yellowbird")	5-7-45	1982	*Self-taught, with some help from aunt:* Lucy Martinez *and sister:* Florence A. Naranjo	*Mother:* Rosalie Aguilar *Father:* Jose A. Aguilar *Sisters:* Annie Martinez Kathy Trujillo *Brother:* Alfred Aguilar

SANTA CLARA

Dorothy and Paul Gutierrez (wife and husband)	Dorothy, 9-17-40	ca. 1978	*Paul's aunt:* Margaret Gutierrez	*Sons:* Paul Gutierrez, Jr. Gary Gutierrez
	Paul, 12-1-36	ca. 1978	*Paul's sister* Pauline Naranjo	*Paul's father:* Luther Gutierrez *Paul's grandparents:* Lela and Van Gutierrez *Niece:* Stephanie Naranjo

> "In my family we started in pottery early. I began making pottery and figurines when I was about age five. My mother died when I was six, but my father, Abristo Naranjo, who was a famous potter, and my aunt, Lusina Baca, taught me. My daughter, Martha Mirabal, started early, too — about age six, and my granddaughter, Tammie Mirabal, has been doing unpolished Nativities and figurines since she was four."
>
> **Maria I. Naranjo**
> **Santa Clara**

Name of Artist	Date of Birth	Date of First Storyteller	Person Who Taught Artist Pottery Making	Potters in the Artist's Family
Margaret and Luther Gutierrez (sister and brother team)	Margaret, 12-16-36 Luther, 12-12-11	1970s	*Parents:* Lela and Van Gutierrez	*Luther's son:* Paul Gutierrez *Luther's daughter:* Pauline Naranjo *Luther's granddaughter:* Stephanie Naranjo *Grandsons:* Paul Gutierrez, Jr. Gary Gutierrez, Jr.
Martha Mirabal	7-4-46	ca. 1979	*Mother:* Maria I. Naranjo	*Daughter:* Tammie Mirabal *Son:* James Mirabal
Maria I. Naranjo	10-21-19	1968	*Father:* Abristo Naranjo *Aunt:* Lusina Baca	*Sister:* Isabel Naranjo *Daughter:* Martha Mirabal *Granddaughter:* Tammie Mirabal *Grandson:* James Mirabal

Tiwa Pueblos

Name of Artist	Date of Birth	Date of First Storyteller	Person Who Taught Artist Pottery Making	Potters in the Artist's Family
TAOS				
Juanita Martinez	2-18-46	1979	*Mother:* Katherine Waquie	*Sister:* Clarita Romero *Cousin:* Santana Seonia
ISLETA				
Ramona Blythe	10-15-60	1984	*Mother:* Stella Teller	*Grandmother:* Felicita Jojolla *Sisters:* Chris Lucero Lynette Teller
Chris Lucero	1-10-56	1982	*Mother:* Stella Teller	*Grandmother:* Felicita Jojolla *Sisters:* Ramona Blythe Lynette Teller
Lynette Teller	8-21-63	1983	*Mother:* Stella Teller	*Grandmother:* Felicita Jojolla *Sisters:* Ramona Blythe Chris Lucero
Stella Teller	2-10-29	1978	*Mother:* Felicita Jojolla	*Grandmother:* Emilia Lente Carpio *Great-grandmother:* Marcellina Jojolla *Daughters:* Ramona Blythe Chris Lucero Lynette Teller

Zuni Pueblo

Name of Artist	Date of Birth	Date of First Storyteller	Person Who Taught Artist Pottery Making	Potters in the Artist's Family
Nellie Bica	ca. 1904	ca. 1917	*Aunt*	*Daughter:* Quanita Kalestewa *Granddaughters:* Erma Kalestewa Rowena Kalestewa Connie Yatsayte
Jennie Laate	9-26-33	1978	*Grandmother:* Dolores Stein *Mother:* Frances Abeita	*Sister:* Louise Amos *Daughter:* Maggie Laate
Josephine Nahohai	7-20-12	1960s	*Aunt:* "Lonkeena"	*Mother:* "La Wa Ta" *Granddaughter*
Anderson Peynetsa	2-14-69	1982	*Teacher at school:* Jennie Laate	*None*

"The story behind the owl figure, as my uncle told me, was that the owl is the protector of the night. Long ago, when neighboring tribes were about to attack the Zunis, the owl, through his hooting, warned the Zunis that the enemies were around, so then the Zunis got prepared. The owl figure reminds the Zunis that the owl is always on the lookout for your family and making sure that your family is safe."

Josephine Nahohai
Zuni

Listed below are 130 artists who are known to
other figurative pieces, but whom we we.
various reasons: a few were deceased, many we
despite repeated efforts, and some came to our a

*Indicates family member of artists documented in the survey.

Keres Pueblos

Cochiti

Juanita Arquero*
Sara Arquero
Magdalena (Maggie) Chalan*
Denise Edwards
Felicita Eustace
Delfino (Butch) Herrera
Dorothy Herrera
Francis Herrera
Laurencita Herrera*
Mary Frances Herrera
Trinidad Herrera
Patricia Lewis*
Mary Lewis*
Guadalupe Ortiz
Inez Ortiz
Angel Quintana*
Margaret Quintana
Patricia Romero
Teresita Romero*
B. Suina
Catharine Suina
Esther Suina
Louise E. Suina
Maria Suina*
Patty Suina*
Elizabeth Trujillo
Felicita Trujillo
Marianita Venado*

Acoma

Wanda Aleno
C. Garcia
Rose Chino Garcia
William Garcia
Loretta Joe
Lucy Juanico
Marie S. Juanico
Dolores Lewis

Anita Lowden
Rebecca Lucario
Sara Martinez
Charmae Natseway
Mamie Ortiz*
Stella Shutiva
Marjorie Valdo
M. Wacquie

San Felipe

Sharon Chavez

The Towa Pueblo of Jemez

Reyes Madalena Butler
Gabriel Casiquito Cajero*
Frances Casiquito*
Ramona Chiana
Rebecca Coonsis
Glendora and Dennis Daubs
Gordon Foley*
Juanita Fragua*
Laura Fragua
Virginia Fragua*
Bertha Gachupin*
Joseph Gachupin*
Darlene Loretto
Linda Lucero
Mary Madalena*
Emily Montoya
Nora Padilla
Irwin Louis Pecos*
Jackie Pecos*
Stephanie Pecos*
Clarita Romero*
Mary Small
Sandy Suina
Christine Toledo

Dorelia Toledo
Lucy Toledo
Sefora Y. Tosa
Antonita Toya*
Camilla Toya*
Damian Toya*
Eloise Toya
Mary Rose Toya
Norma Toya
Robert Toya
Mary S. Tsosie
Angela Wacquie
Felipa C. Wacquie
Katherine Waquie*
Kathleen Wall*

Pula Gutierrez
Linda Halsey
James Mirabal*
Tammie Mirabal*
Nora Naranjo-Morse
Abristo Naranjo*
Flora Naranjo
Joe Naranjo
Madeline Naranjo
Margaret Naranjo
Pauline Naranjo*
Clara Stone
Mary Agnes Tafoya
Crescencia Tafoya
Dorothy Tsosie

Tewa Pueblos

Tesuque

Anna Marie Lovato*
Alice Vigil
Eliza Ruth Vigil*
Art Vigil*

Nambe

Dorothy Gutierrez
Virginia Gutierrez*
OQA
Carmen Robinson

San Juan

Gordon Garcia*

San Ildefonso

Blue Corn
Isabel and Raymond Gonzales
Florence Naranjo*
Enke Pena
Juan Tafoya

Santa Clara

Marie Askan
Cactus Flower
Jody Falwell
Gary Gutierrez*
Paul Gutierrez, Jr.*

Tiwa Pueblos

Taos

Antoinette Concha*
Delfino Concha, Jr.*
John Concha*
Justin Concha*
Monica Concha*
Renee Concha*
Vernon Concha*
Cheyenne Jim
Bernie Naranjo

Isleta

Margie Zuni

Zuni Pueblo

Myra Eriacho
Erma Kalestewa*
Quanita Kalestewa*
Rowena Kalestewa*
Connie Yatsayte*

Hopi Pueblos

Caroline and Preston Duwyenie

PART IV

Reference Material

Notes

1. This statement and those which follow in quotation marks in this section were, unless otherwise indicated, made by Helen Cordero in conversations with Barbara Babcock between 1978 and 1984.

2. Nampeyo is associated with the revival (about 1895) of the prehistoric Sikyatki Polychrome style at Hano, a First Mesa village in the Hopi country of northeastern Arizona. This style was inspired by pottery excavated under the direction of anthropologist J. Walter Fewkes at Sikyatki, a site at which Nampeyo's husband, Lesou, was a fieldworker. For further information, see Frisbie (1973). As Brody (1979: 605) has pointed out, "Nampeyo's combination of superior craftsmanship with an appropriate antique model was the prototype for art pottery revivals at other Pueblos and set the pattern for twentieth-century Hopi art pottery." The other major art pottery revival began in the years following 1907, when Dr. Edgar L. Hewett began archaeological excavation on the Pajarito Plateau and Kenneth Chapman encouraged the women of San Ildefonso Pueblo to re-create this traditional pottery. By 1915 Maria and Julian Martinez had attained a skill that surpassed the others; in 1919 Julian Martinez developed the technique for producing black-on-black ware; and by 1925, almost all of the San Ildefonso potters were making this type of pottery. For further information see Marriott (1948), Spivey (1979), and Peterson (1977).

3. The word *pueblo* is Spanish in origin and is used in two senses in this text. First, pueblo is a synonym for the English word *village*, as, for example, in Cochiti Pueblo or the Pueblo of Cochiti; this usage is a direct translation from one of its Spanish meanings. Second, Pueblo refers to a culture or way of life shared in common by certain village-dwelling Native Americans in the Southwest, specifically, the nineteen Pueblo villages of New Mexico and the Hopi communities of northern Arizona. For further discussion of cultural commonalities and shared identity, despite linguistic diversity among these communities, see Dozier (1970) and Ortiz (1976). Five different languages are spoken (with dialect differences) among the nineteen New Mexico Pueblos: KERES is the language spoken at Cochiti, Santo Domingo, San Felipe, Santa Ana, Zia, Laguna, and Acoma; Jemez is the only TOWA-speaking Pueblo; San Juan, Santa Clara, San Ildefonso, Pojoaque, Nambe, and Tesuque speak TEWA; Taos, Picuris, Sandia, and Isleta speak TIWA; and ZUNI is the language of Zuni Pueblo. For discussion of the Pueblo capacity for revitalization, the dynamics of cultural survival, and the

importance of Pueblo art, especially pottery, as a symbol of cultural identity, see Ortiz (1976) and Brody (1976, 1979).

4. For discussion of Puebloan prehistory, see Dozier (1970), Longacre (1970), Ford *et al*. (1972), and Ortiz, ed. (1979: 22–161). For discussion of the necessity of pottery to the development of Pueblo culture and of its symbolic significance, see Cushing (1886, 1920).

5. For further discussion of the importance of pottery in Pueblo culture, see Brody (1976, 1979), Ortiz (1976), Bunzel (1972), Hardin (1983), and Babcock (I: 1984, 1986b).

6. The earliest pottery found in the Southwest dates from 500 B.C. to 300 B.C. and occurs in the Hohokam and Mogollon cultures of Arizona and New Mexico. By 200 A.D. to 300 A.D., pottery technology had spread to the Anasazi culture of the Four Corners area. The Anasazi, who are regarded as the ancestors of present-day Pueblo people, reached their highest development between 1100 A.D. and 1300 A.D. Anasazi borrowings from the Mogollon are evident and numerous, and, while the Hohokam tradition is outside the area of the eventual development of prehistoric Pueblo culture, cross influences are obvious, as are the borrowings from and trading with Casas Grandes.

7. See Cushing (1883), Kirk (1943), and Branson (1976) for discussion and illustration of fetishes, especially Zuni.

8. Hammack (1974: 33).

9. For discussion and illustration of Mimbres painted pottery, see Brody (1977a, 1977b) and Brody, Scott, and LeBlanc (1983).

10. See Morss (1954) for detailed description of the temporal and spatial distribution of prehistoric figurines. Useful summary discussions of the figurine complex in the Southwest are also to be found in Tanner (1976) and Haury (1978).

11. Morss (1954: 27).

12. For detailed and comprehensive analysis and illustration of Hohokam figurines, see Haury (1937, 1978).

13. See Morss (1954) for illustration and discussion of "babe-in-cradle" handles and Hammack (1974) for representative illustrations and a summary discussion of prehistoric effigy vessels.

14. For discussion and illustration of Casas Grandes effigy vessels, of trading networks, and of iconographic resemblances to both prehistoric and historic Pueblo pottery designs, see DiPeso (1974, vol. 2; 1977).

15. Haury (1978: 266).

16. See especially "The Function of Figurines," pp. 53–63 in Morss (1954); for discussion of the "toy vs. fetish" controversy among both archaeologists and anthropologists, also see Bullen (1948).

17. For discussion of Pueblo ceremonialism and description or illustration of altars and sacred objects, see Parsons (1933, 1939), Cushing (1883, 1886, 1920), Bunzel (1932), Stevenson (1894), Curtis (1976, vol. 16), and White (1932a, 1932b, 1935, 1942). There is abundant archaeological evidence that figurative pottery, especially miniatures, is also associated with mortuary rituals and is buried with the deceased. The Spanish clergy discouraged these practices, but various ethnographic remarks attest to their persistence in the historic period. See especially Dumarest (1918), Parsons (1939), and Nequatewa (1939).

18. Discussions of the meanings of ceramic figurative designs and objects are scattered and various. See Parsons (1919, 1939), Cushing (1883, 1886, 1920), Spinden (1931), Bunzel (1932, 1972), Coolidge (1929), Chapman (1950), and Hardin (1983). In her introduction to *Pueblo Indian Religion* (1939: xi), Parsons remarked that all forms of Pueblo art, "whatever else they are, also are measures to invoke and coerce, to gratify or pay, the Spirits." And, in his classic essay of post-Spanish pottery (1950: 6), Kenneth Chapman observed that "through the three centuries that have passed, the designs of Pueblo pottery have had one dominant theme, a prayer for rain for the

maturing crops, a matter of gravest concern in this semi-arid region where the menace of drought is ever in mind. So in endless profusion of combinations appear the symbols of mountains and clouds, lightning and rain, and leaves, flowers, and seed pods as emblems of growth and maturity. With these frequently appear fantastic forms of birds or the feathers of birds, both of which serve to bear their prayers aloft."

19. Cushing (1886: 510–515).

20. Hardin (1983: 33).

21. In addition to the summary statements of Pueblo origin myths made by Parsons (1939), see Cushing (1896, 1920), Stirling (1942), White (1932a, 1932b, 1935, 1962), Boas (1928), Benedict (1931), and Sebag (1971). The motif of creation through the molding of meal, dust, or clay is not limited to origin myths, but is widely found throughout Pueblo narratives.

22. Parsons (1939: 336). For further discussion of the *cacique*'s "children" and associated beliefs and practices among the Keresan Pueblos, see White (1932b, 1935, 1962), Lange (1968), Lange and Riley, eds. (1966), and Lange, Riley, and Lange, eds. (1975).

23. Parsons (1929–1930: 279). For additional discussion of objects and rites of increase, see Parsons (1918, 1919, 1939), Dumarest (1918), White (1932b, 1935, 1942), and Fewkes (1906). Because of their similarity to Catholic practices associated with both Christmas and All Saints Day, and because these rituals of increase as observed earlier in this century involved *santu* worship, Parsons and others have questioned whether or not they are Spanish in origin. There is no doubt that there has been Catholic influence and that Pueblo religious practices have been characterized by what Robin Fox has aptly described as "accretion"; there is also considerable and widespread archaeological evidence of similar figurines and practices in pre-Spanish times.

24. Personal communication, Florence Hawley Ellis, July 1980; Doris Monthan, transcript of interview with Juana Leno, February 1977.

25. Dumarest (1918: 141).

26. Parsons (1939: 574).

27. See Bandelier (1890–1892) and Bolton (1916) for a summary of and quotations from early Spanish accounts by Espejo, Villagran, Onate, and de Sosa concerning the "*muchos idolos*" found among the Indians of New Mexico.

28. For further discussion and illustration of Hawikuh effigies and figurines, see Hodge (1924, 1942), Parsons (1919: 282), and Smith, Woodbury, and Woodbury (1966: plates 26, 27). See Kidder (1932: 113–151) for discussion and illustration of Pecos figurines.

29. Between 1875 and 1881, Reverend Sheldon Jackson and Colonel James Stevenson collected figurative pottery from Acoma, Laguna, Cochiti, Santo Domingo, Zia, Santa Clara, San Ildefonso, and Tesuque, in addition to Hopi and Zuni. Then, as in the 1980s, most of Hopi's figurative genius was expressed in wood, rather than clay, in their famous carved kachina dolls. For discussion and illustration of kachina dolls, see Fewkes (1903), Colton (1949), Dockstader (1954), and Wright (1977, 1984). For discussion and illustration of a few Hopi Polacca Polychrome effigies and figurines made between 1870 and 1890, see Wade (1980).

30. Holmes (1889: 320).

31. Dozier (1907: 6, 9–10).

32. Dutton (1948: 45). In his entry on Tesuque in *Southwestern Indian Tribes* (1968), Tom Bahti has equally negative things to say about Rain Gods.

33. In Greenhalgh and Megaw (1978: 75).

34. In addition to Haeberlin (1916), see especially Cushing (1920) and Benedict (1934) for discussion of fertility as the dominant idea or master trope of Pueblo culture.

35. In other essays (I: 1982a and 1986a), I have suggested that these ceramic caricatures are not simply portraits of whitemen, but portraits of portraits of white-

men — i.e., representations of Pueblo clowns dressed up and behaving as whitemen. For further discussion of Pueblo clowning, see Ortiz (1972, 1976), Hieb (1972), and Babcock (II: 1982,1984).

36. Church (1959: 65).

37. Benedict (1931: xi). See also Benedict's letter of September 5, 1925, from Cochiti to Margaret Mead, in Mead (1973: 300).

38. For discussion and illustration of Helen Cordero's Nativities, see Monthan and Monthan (1979: Frontispiece and pp. 26–30).

39. Like many other Pueblo potters, Helen Cordero always uses the English plural noun, "potteries," rather than the proper collective noun, "pottery." From the native point of view, the latter usage is inconceivable, for each piece of pottery is a being with a unique existence. In the remainder of this essay, I, too, use potteries without quotation marks.

40. See Harlow (1977: 50) for illustration of the Nightcrier and his nineteenth-century friend.

41. See Monthan and Monthan (1979: 31–34) for description and illustration of one of Ada Suina's Nativities. For a photographic study of Ada firing her Storytellers, see Edward Klamm, "The Potter's Art," in SWAIA's 1983 Indian Market Program, pp. 24–26.

42. For discussion and illustration of a Frances Suina Nativity, see Monthan and Monthan (1979: 34–36).

43. A Felipa Trujillo Nativity is illustrated and discussed in Monthan and Monthan (1979: 40–42).

44. See Monthan and Monthan (1979: 37–39) for discussion and illustration of a Dorothy Trujillo Nativity.

45. Here and elsewhere in my discussion, I have used the word "style" in Meyer Schapiro's sense to refer to "the constant form — and sometimes the constant elements, qualities, and expression — in the art of an individual or group" (Schapiro 1953: 287). As he notes, and as the styles of particular Pueblos demonstrate, "it is easy to imagine a decided change in material, technique, or subject matter accompanied by little change in the basic form. . . . A style is like a language, with an internal order and expressiveness, admitting a varied intensity or delicacy of statement" (289, 291). Cochiti Polychrome has, for over a century, been distinguished not only by its creamy white slip and stone-polished red base, but its combination of geometric designs with ceremonial figurative designs associated with rain and fruition. As Frank and Harlow (1974: 77) have noted, "a whole world of Pueblo religious motifs can be seen" on Cochiti pottery. Harlow also points out that "a typical Cochiti feature is the habit of embellishing the encircling framing lines with pendent figures" — a habit which persists in inverted, three-dimensional form in the Storyteller. In addition to making more figurines and effigy vessels than other Pueblos, Cochiti potters have also been inclined to appliqué small figures, lizards in particular, to their bowls and jars. The Cochiti style of figurative design, both two- and three-dimensional, has frequently been described as "crude," "haphazard," "spidery," "fussy," and "grotesque."

46. For discussion of miniaturization with commercialization, see Graburn (1976:*passim*); of Pueblo pottery in particular, see Chapters 3 and 5, by Brody and Gill. For discussion of miniatures in prehistoric and historic Pueblo ceramics, see especially Bullen (1948) and Nequatewa (1939).

47. For extensive discussion and illustration of traditional firing methods, see Guthe (1925) and Lambert (1966b). Harlow (1977) and Spivey (1976) also have useful summary discussions. For photographs of a typical, traditional firing of Storytellers, see Klamm (1983).

48. Few, if any, Cochiti potters exhibit and sell at the Eight Northern Pueblos Arts and Crafts Fair for the simple reason that it is usually held the weekend after Cochiti Feast, July 14, and most potters have been too busy with preparation for the feast to

make enough pottery both for that fair and for Indian Market, which usually occurs the third weekend in August.

49. This total count is as accurate as possible, but, nonetheless, approximate for several reasons: (1) new Storyteller potters are constantly emerging and do not always sign their own names, but that of a mother, sister, or aunt already well known for Storytellers; (2) many individuals make other figures, but not Storytellers per se; and (3) many more potters produce and show Storytellers once or twice and are never heard from again. We have, however, interviewed in person, by phone, or by letter-questionnaire over one hundred potters who are consistently producing Storytellers and other figurative forms.

50. For further information regarding Pueblo affiliation by marriage and relatives in other Pueblos making Storytellers, see Part III.

51. For centuries Pueblo pottery making has followed a pattern of community specialization in terms of shapes and types of pottery as well as distinctive styles, designs, and types and colors of paint. As Margaret Hardin (1983) has noted, among Pueblo potters "stylistic screens" are very well established and well developed, and the practice of taking a shape or a design from another Pueblo and translating it into the local style is quite common. For useful summaries of the types, shapes, and styles of ceramics associated with the New Mexico Pueblos, see Spivey (1976), Toulouse (1977), Frank and Harlow (1974), and Harlow (1977). See Wobst (1977) for an interesting discussion of style, information exchange, and social or cultural boundaries.

52. See Monthan and Monthan (1979: 46–48) for discussion and illustration of an Ethel Shields Nativity.

53. For discussion and illustration of a Juana Leno Nativity, see Monthan and Monthan (1979: 43–45).

54. During the 1970s and 1980s, very little pottery at all was produced at the Keres Pueblos of San Felipe, Santa Ana, and Laguna. See Gill (1976) for a discussion of Laguna pottery and the consequence of acculturation. Zia was long famous among the Pueblos for its fine, large, water jars, but the manufacture of these jars declined after the coming of the railroads and the introduction of commercial utility ware. However, Halseth's and Chapman's assistance was successful in reviving the old pottery, and in the 1970s and 1980s, Zia potters once again began to produce fine bowls and jars with the distinctive Zia bird design. Chapman's efforts at revival were less successful at Santo Domingo, and relatively few potters produced pottery there, where jewelry-making became the major craft industry. And, as previously noted, the making of figurative pottery for sale has long been prohibited at Santo Domingo. For further information and a chronological survey of trends in Pueblo pottery making in the twentieth century, see Harlow (1977) and Toulouse (1977).

55. Toulouse (1977: 52).

56. See Monthan and Monthan (1979: 49–51) for discussion and illustration of a Marie Romero Nativity.

57. For discussion and illustration of an Alma Concha Nativity produced while she was living and working at Taos Pueblo, see Monthan and Monthan (1979: 77–80).

58. For discussion and illustration of the different types of Rain Gods produced at Tesuque in the last century, see Gratz (1976).

59. See Harlow (1977: 47) for color illustration of three different styles of Rain Gods; see Toulouse (1977: 41) for other examples of Tesuque figurine and curio ware from the 1900–1920 era.

60. See Toulouse (1977: 62–63) for examples of figures by Martin Vigil similar to those for which he won a prize at the 1926 Indian Market.

61. See Monthan and Monthan (1979: 13–25) for discussion and illustration of several different Manuel Vigil Nativities.

62. For discussion and illustration of a Reycita Garcia Nativity, see Monthan and Monthan (1979: 64–66). Reycita's first Nativities were made in the 1960s.

63. One of Alfred Aguilar's Nativities is illustrated and discussed in Monthan and Monthan (1979: x, 61–63).

64. For discussion and illustration of both redware and blackware Nativities by Maria I. Naranjo, see Monthan and Monthan (1979: 73–76).

65. Ibid.: 73.

66. A red and buff Nativity by Dorothy Gutierrez is illustrated and discussed in Monthan and Monthan (1979: 67–69).

67. For discussion and illustration of a characteristic polychrome Nativity by Margaret and Luther Gutierrez, see Monthan and Monthan (1979: 70–72).

68. We have not included examples of Nora Naranjo-Morse's work, both because she does not in any sense make traditional Storytellers and because we were not able to locate any of the very few mother-and-child figures that she has produced.

69. Harlow (1977: 21).

70. Stevenson (1883: 365–66).

71. Hardin (1983: 38). For illustration of several Zuni owls made during the past century, see Hardin (1983: 27, 38, 39).

72. Ortiz (1977: 9).

73. Silko (1977: 2).

74. Silko (1981a: 59).

75. Ricoeur (1983: 30). Annette Weiner's "model of reproduction" is relevant to the present discussion. This model is based on the premise that "any society must reproduce and regenerate certain elements of value in order for the society to continue. . . . These elements of value include human beings, social relations, cosmological phenomena such as ancestors, and resources such as land, material objects, names, and body decorations" (Weiner 1980: 71). This model has been elaborated and refined in her more recent formulation of the configuration of "elementary cycling," which consists of "components associated with a primary encoding of sex, gender, and time" (Weiner 1982: 9). Whatever else it may be, Helen Cordero's Storyteller is a "model of reproduction" and an exemplary embodiment of "elementary cycling."

Glossary

(Terms associated with Pueblo pottery used within the context of this book)

Appliqué. Decoration or ornamentation created by attaching modeled clay forms or fillets to the surface of vessels or figurines. This mode of ornamentation, with or without painted design, is common in Pueblo ceramics from the earliest to the most recent.

Band. A horizontal encircling area of design which is usually bounded by *framing* or *banding lines,* sometimes broken with a short *ceremonial gap.* The band may or may not be partitioned into distinct sections or *panels.*

Black-on-black. A type of pottery invented at San Ildefonso in 1919 and still produced there and at Santa Clara in the mid-1980s in which designs are delineated by matte paint on a polished background. The black color is the result of carbonization, produced by firing in a reducing atmosphere.

Black-on-white. Black paint on a white slip. A style of painting common in both Anasazi and Mogollon prehistoric pottery and characteristic of Acoma historic pottery in particular.

Blackware. Any type of black pottery, plain, carved, polished, or decorated, produced primarily at Santa Clara and San Ildefonso. Red clay used to make blackware turns black from carbonization, produced by a reducing atmosphere.

Bowl. A vessel with an opening at approximately the greatest width. Large bowls usually used for mixing bread dough are called *dough bowls.*

Canteen. A small vessel, with a relatively narrow neck and a pair of handles, made for carrying water.

Carbon paint (organic, vegetal paint). A black-firing pigment made by boiling leaves and stems of certain plants to a thick, brown juice. When made from Rocky Mountain Bee Plant, carbon paint is called *guaco.*

Ceremonial break (line break, spirit path). An interruption or break in an encircling design. A recurrent feature in painted design on both prehistoric and traditional historic vessels. In traditional belief, a break is left for the source of life. Closing the lines is thought to have a negative effect on the life and health of the potter.

Ceremonial vessel. A pot with a special form or designs that denote association with Pueblo religious ceremonies. Stair-step sculpture of the rim is common on ceremonial bowls and jars. Painted designs often include cloud, rain, lightning, corn plant, and feather symbols as well as realistic depictions of plumed serpents, frogs, dragonflies, and other water creatures. Many of these designs have been common on pottery made for sale at Cochiti.

Clay. A mineral substance of fine texture which becomes plastic when wet and can be variously shaped. Once mixed with temper and fired, it becomes hard and relatively immune to softening again with water. Clay is used by Pueblo potters for the body of a vessel, for covering the surface (see *slip*), and for paint to decorate the surface.

Coil-and-scrape (coiling). A method of forming pottery, common to Pueblo groups, by building up the walls with ropelike coils of clay and then scraping them to a uniform thickness. In contrast, some other Southwestern groups build up a vessel with slabs and use a paddle-and-anvil to thin the walls.

Composite figure. A figure or effigy vessel with other smaller figures appliquéd to its surface. Both animal and human Storytellers are composite figures.

Corrugated. A type of pottery made by leaving the coils unobliterated on the exterior surface of the pot, and sometimes indenting the coils to produce a simple design. Corrugated ware was common in Mogollon and Anasazi prehistoric pottery and reached a peak in Pueblo III (1100–1300 A.D.)

Curing. Once raw clay is pounded, ground, and sifted, it is mixed with enough water to make it plastic, temper is added, and it is kneaded, set aside, and kept damp for a curing period before use.

Design. An overall scheme of decoration, composed of various motifs, each being made of one or more elements.

Effigy (effigy vessel). A primary vessel (bowl, jar, pitcher) wholly or partially shaped into a three-dimensional life form, sometimes used for ceremonial purposes.

Elements. The simplest, minimal parts of a design or motif with which the entire pattern is constructed.

Engraving (sgraffito). Scratching through the slip of a fired clay object to produce a decoration by exposing the color of the clay beneath the slip.

Fetish. Any object used for religious or ceremonial purposes. More specifically, small, zoomorphic figures carved from wood or stone or modeled from clay.

Figurative pottery. All ceramics, whether figurines or effigy vessels, shaped into recognizable life forms. In Pueblo pottery these forms may be representations of deities, humans, animals, and vegetables.

Figurine. A free-standing, three-dimensional animal or human figure. Depending on size, ceramic figurines may be solid or hollow, but they are not vessels. Figurative vessels are referred to as *effigy vessels* or simply *effigies.*

Fire cloud. A carbon smudge on the surface of a pot, usually caused by the incomplete burning of a piece of dung fuel that has fallen against the pot. Fire clouds were once considered blemishes, and most potters try to avoid them. However, given the proliferation of nontraditional methods, collectors in the 1980s regarded them as positive proof of traditional firing.

Firing. The heating process in which clay forms are hardened. Traditional technique uses cedar (juniper) wood and an "oven" of dung cakes. A *reducing* fire excludes fresh air and oxygen from the center, resulting in pottery that is a gray tone of white; the color becomes black if the fire is deliberately smothered with pulverized manure. An *oxidizing* fire allows fresh air to permeate to the center, so that the fuel burns cleanly and without smoke. An *oxidizing* atmosphere is necessary for the firing of all types of pottery except blackware.

Framing (banding) lines. *See* **Band.**

Glaze paint. A finely powdered mineral substance (such as lead oxide mixed with copper, iron, or manganese) painted on vessel surfaces which melts in firing and becomes glossy. Pueblo glazes were always decorative and not applied as an overall coating for waterproofing. After about 1700, glaze paint was abandoned in favor of matte paint.

"Grandma Clay" (Mother Clay, Clay Old Woman). The ancestor spirit who is the guardian of clay and the primal teacher of pottery making. Traditional potters "talk to her" and give her cornmeal to thank her for her help at every stage of the pottery-making process, from taking her "flesh" to firing.

Guaco. A vegetal paint, widely used by Pueblo potters, produced by boiling Rocky Mountain Bee Plant (*cleome serrulata*), or "wild spinach," into a sludge which hardens into a cake that is moistened for use.

Historic pottery. Pottery produced after the arrival of Spaniards in the Southwest. While *historic* refers in general to pottery made between 1600 A.D. and the present, it is usually used to refer to pottery made between 1600 and 1920. Pottery made after 1920, with the institution of Indian Market and revivals in various Pueblos, is usually referred to as *modern* or *contemporary*. For division of the Historic Period into subperiods, see Harlow (1977) and Toulouse (1977).

Incising. Scratching the surface of a clay form with a pointed instrument while the clay is still damp to produce decorations.

Jars. Vessels, usually taller than bowls, with a much narrower opening than their greatest width. *Storage jars* are large vessels (larger than twelve inches in height or diameter) with a narrow opening used traditionally for the storage of grain and other dry materials. *Wedding vases* or *jars* are smaller jars with two necks and openings, connected by a handle.

Matte paint. A mineral or vegetal substance used to decorate pottery, which is not vitrified or glossy after firing; the opposite of glaze paint and the common mode of Pueblo pottery decoration.

Micaceous clay. Clay containing flakes of mica which produces pottery with a glittery surface, the color of burnished bronze. Some potters use micaceous clay for the slip or for accent paint, but not for the vessel body.

Mineral paint. Paint made from inorganic compounds, such as hematite, and usually mixed with vegetal-based material to aid in adherence to the surface of the pot.

Modeled. Formation of a desired shape by manipulation of a lump of clay with the fingers. Also referred to as the *pinch* method. An entire vessel (usually small) may be modeled, or modeled appliqué(s) may be attached to the primary form, as in Cochiti lizard pots or Storytellers.

Modern (contemporary) pottery. Pueblo pottery made after 1920, after the institution of Indian Market (1922), and after revivals in pottery-producing Pueblos.

Motif. A recognizable and characteristic part of an overall design, composed of one or several elements. For example, the rain-cloud motif on Cochiti pottery.

Mono. Spanish word meaning "monkey, silly fool, mimic, mere doll." A term widely used by dealers and collectors until the late 1960s to refer to all ceramic figurines. The term was very rarely used by potters themselves.

Negative design. A design (e.g., a negative leaf design) in which the amount of painted area (usually black) exceeds that of the amount of visible background area (cream, buff, or red). Negative design is quite common on Cochiti and Santo Domingo pottery.

Nontraditional pottery. Pottery made by other than traditional methods, such as by using potter's wheels, molds, gas or electric kiln firing, or by using commercial, rather than natural, clays or paints. The term is also sometimes used to refer to other than traditional shapes (ashtrays, candlesticks, etc.) or subjects (white men, railroad cars, automobiles, etc.). Some pottery (particularly at Acoma, Jemez, and Tesuque Pueblos during the 1980s) has been made using a combination of traditional and nontraditional methods. The "Non-Traditional" category at Indian Market includes shape and subject as well as method of manufacture.

***Olla* (water jar).** A medium-sized vessel (from eight to twelve inches tall), with shoulders and a neck, and often with a concave base to facilitate carrying. Traditionally used for carrying and storing water.

Oxidizing atmosphere. *See* **Firing.**

Panel. A rectangular division of a design band, usually created by vertical lines connecting the upper and lower framing lines of a band.

Polishing. The process of rubbing the dried slip of a pot with a smooth, worn stone or a piece of leather or cloth to a smooth, lustrous finish.

Pottery (ceramics). Earthenware. Modeled clay that has been hardened by firing. Anglos use the collective nouns, pottery and ceramics, interchangeably. From the native point of view, such a collective term is inconceivable, and older Pueblo potters use the Pueblo English term "potteries."

Polychrome. The use of three or more colors on the painted surface of a pot. Most traditional polychrome is black, red (or terra-cotta), and cream (or buff).

Poster paint. A water-based, fugitive paint introduced by Anglos in the 1920s and applied after firing. Also called *showcard colors*. Few potters used actual poster paint by 1986, but the term has been used generically for any commercial paint applied after firing, such as the *acrylic* paints popular in the 1980s.

Prehistoric pottery. Pottery produced by southwestern Native Americans prior to the arrival of Spaniards in the Southwest in the sixteenth century.

Red-on-buff (red-on-tan). A type of pottery characterized by red or terra-cotta painted designs on a buff or tan ground. This particular two-color scheme is favored by the Loretto sisters of Jemez Pueblo.

Red-on-red. A type of pottery popular at Santa Clara in which designs are delineated by means of a dull (matte) terra-cotta paint on a polished terra-cotta slipped surface. If the piece is fired in an oxidizing atmosphere, the result is red-on-red, matte-and-polish pottery; a reducing atmosphere produces black-on-black.

Redware. Pottery made of a red clay and fired in an oxidizing atmosphere. The same clay fired in a reducing atmosphere produces blackware.

Reducing atmosphere. *See* **Firing.**

Rocky mountain bee plant. *See* ***Guaco.***

Sanding. A process which involves rubbing a dry, scraped pot with a pumice stone or sandpaper to prepare the surface for slipping and final polishing.

Scraping. The process of smoothing over the coils used in the construction of a pot and to evening out the walls by removing excess clay; frequently done with a gourd, a wet rag, or a knife.

Sherd (shard, potsherd). Broken pieces of pottery sometimes ground and used as *temper*. Designs are often inspired by these fragments found in ruins.

Slip. Clay which is thinned with water to a creamy consistency and applied with a rag or sponge to pottery surfaces as decoration, as a base for decoration, or to hide imperfections in the clay body. The slip may be polished or left as a matte finish.

Style. A unique method of composition with a distinctive combination of elements. In Schapiro's (1953) terms, "the constant form — and sometimes constant elements, qualities, and expression — in the art of an individual or group."

Temper. Any coarse, nonplastic material that is added to clay to facilitate workability and even drying. Temper is necessary to lessen temperature shock and breakage in the quick-firing process. Common tempers are sand, ground sherds, and ground volcanic rock.

Terra-cotta. Red earthenware clay, some varieties of which are used for shaping vessels; other varieties are used for painted design.

Textured. Having a pattern produced by punching, incising, engraving, or otherwise manipulating the clay surface.

Tourist ware or **pottery (curio, souvenir pottery).** Commercial pottery produced after 1880, primarily for sale to visitors to the Southwest. Although the tourist market has furnished the basic financial support for the production of Indian pottery since 1880, the term has disparaging connotations and generally denotes small, simple pots, sometimes made in nontraditional shapes and by nontraditional methods.

Type. The designation given to a group of pots that have a majority of characteristics in common — for example, Cochiti Polychrome, Santa Clara Black, Jemez Red-on-buff, etc.

Utility ware. Pottery traditionally made for everyday use, such as cooking, eating, storage, and water carrying. Archaeologists commonly use this term to describe pottery that is undecorated except for indentations.

Vegetal paint. *See* **Carbon paint.**

Yucca. A desert plant (*Yucca glauca*) found throughout the Southwest that has a long, narrow, fibrous leaf. The leaves have been used by traditional Pueblo potters to make paint brushes: leaves were cut to lengths of five to seven inches, one end was chewed (to separate the fibers and form bristles) and then trimmed to form brushes of one to twelve fibers. Some potters have also boiled yucca leaves for use as black (carbon) paint.

Bibliography

I. Pueblo Ceramics

Albuquerque Museum
    1979   *One Space, Three Visions*. Albuquerque: The Albuquerque Museum.

Anonymous
    1973   Helen Cordero. *SWAIA Quarterly* 8:1, p.6.

Anonymous
    1980   The Corderos of Cochiti. *Mission* 47:4, pp. 8–11.

Anonymous
    1981   Storyteller figures to see or shop for in New Mexico. *Sunset Magazine* 166:4, pp. 45–46.

Anthony, Alexander E., Jr.
    1980   Storytellers. *Art West* 3:4, pp. 64–66.

Arnold, David L.
    1982   Pueblo Pottery: 2,000 Years of Artistry. *National Geographic* 162:5, pp. 593–605.

Austin, Mary
    1934   *Indian Pottery of the Rio Grande*. Pasadena: Esto Publishing Co.

Babcock, Barbara A.
    1978   Helen Cordero, The Storyteller Lady. *New Mexico Magazine* 56:12, pp. 6–8.

    1982a   Clay Voices: Invoking, Mocking, Celebrating. *In* Victor Turner, ed., *Celebrations*. Washington, D.C.: Smithsonian Institution Press, pp. 58–76.

    1982b   The Rio Grande Storyteller, Past and Present. In *Cochiti Pueblo Storytellers and Other Pottery Figurines*. Albuquerque: Adobe Gallery.

Babcock, Barbara A. (*cont.*)

1983 Clay Changes: Helen Cordero and the Pueblo Storyteller. *American Indian Art* 8:2, pp. 30–39.

1984 "We're All in There, in the Clay": Stories, Potteries, Identities. *Proceedings of the Eighth Congress of the International Society for Folk Narrative Research*. Bergen, Norway, pp. 29–48.

1986a Pueblo Clowning and Pueblo Clay: From Icon to Caricature in Cochiti Figurative Ceramics, 1875–1900. *Visible Religion* 4.

1986b Modeled Selves: Helen Cordero's "Little People."*In* E. Bruner and V. Turner, eds., *The Anthropology of Experience*. Urbana: University of Illinois Press.

Bahti, Tom

1966 *Southwestern Indian Arts and Crafts*. Las Vegas: K. C. Publications.

Barry, John W.

1981 *American Indian Pottery: An Identification and Value Guide*. Florence, Alabama: Books Americana.

Baylor, Byrd, and Tom Bahti

1972 *When Clay Sings*. New York: Charles Scribner's Sons.

Borhegyi, Stephan F.

1966 America's Oldest Dolls. *Lore* 16:3, pp. 87–91.

Bott, John

1978 The Corderos of Cochiti. *SWAIA Quarterly* 15:4, pp. 4–6.

Brainerd, George W.

1949 Human Effigy Vessels of Pueblo Culture. *The Masterkey* 23:4, pp. 121–124.

Branson, Oscar T.

1976 *Fetishes and Carvings of the Southwest*. Santa Fe: Treasure Chest Publications.

Breternitz, David A., Arthur H. Rohn, Jr., and Elizabeth A. Morris

1974 Prehistoric Ceramics of the Mesa Verde Region. *Museum of Northern Arizona Ceramic Series,* No. 5, Flagstaff.

Brody, J. J.

1976 The Creative Consumer: Survival, Revival, and Invention in Southwest Indian Arts. *In* Nelson Graburn, ed., *Ethnic and Tourist Arts*. Berkeley: University of California Press, pp. 70–84.

1977a Mimbres Art: Sidetracked on the Trail of a Mexican Connection. *American Indian Art* 2:4, pp. 26–31.

1977b *Mimbres Painted Pottery*. Albuquerque: University of New Mexico Press.

1979 Pueblo Fine Arts. *In* Ortiz, ed., *Handbook of North American Indians*, vol. 9. Washington, D.C.: Smithsonian Institution, pp. 603–608.

1980 Review of Susan Peterson, *The Living Tradition of Maria Martinez* and of Richard Spivey, *Maria. American Indian Art* 5:3, pp. 65–69.

Brody, J. J., Catharine J. Scott, and Steven A. LeBlanc
    1983   *Mimbres Pottery: Ancient Art of the American Southwest*. New York: Hudson Hills Press.

Bryan, Bruce
    1963   A Hohokam "Venus." *The Masterkey* 37:3, p. 85.

Bullen, Adelaide Kendall
    1948   Archaeological Theory and Anthropological Fact. *American Antiquity* 13:3, pp. 128–134.

Bunzel, Ruth
    1972   *The Pueblo Potter: A Study of Creative Imagination in Primitive Art*. New York: Dover Publications, Inc. Reprint of 1929 edition: New York, Columbia University Press.

Butterfield, Jody
    1980   Daisy Hooee Nampeyo: Passing the Tradition. *New Mexico Magazine* 58:10, pp. 55–60.

Chapman, Kenneth
    1916   The Evolution of the Bird in Decorative Art. *Art and Archaeology* 4:6, pp. 307–316.
    1922   Life Forms in Pueblo Pottery Decoration. *Art and Archaeology* 13:3, pp. 120–122.
    1923   Casas Grandes Pottery. *Art and Archaeology* 16:1–2, pp. 1–2.
    1927   Post-Spanish Pueblo Pottery. *Art and Archaeology* 23:5, pp. 207–213.
    1928   Bird Forms in Zuni Pottery Decoration. *El Palacio* 24:2, pp. 23–25.
    1931   Indian Pottery. *In* Herbert J. Spinden, ed., *Introduction to American Indian Art*. New York: The Exposition of Indian Tribal Arts, Inc., pp. 3–11.
    1950   *Pueblo Indian Pottery of the Post-Spanish Period*. Santa Fe: School of American Research, Bulletin No. 4.
    1970   *The Pottery of San Ildefonso Pueblo*. Albuquerque: University of New Mexico Press.
    1977   *The Pottery of Santo Domingo: A Detailed Study of Its Decoration*. Albuquerque: University of New Mexico Press.

Cleland, Charles F.
    1980   Yuma Dolls. *American Indian Art* 5:3, pp. 36–41, 71.

Colton, Harold S.
    1953   *Potsherds: An Introduction to the Study of Prehistoric Southwestern Ceramics and Their Use in Historic Reconstruction*. Flagstaff: Museum of Northern Arizona.

Cordero, Helen
    1975   The Way of the Na'wa'ya'thitse. *Studio Potter* 4:1, p. 41.

Cushing, Frank Hamilton
    1883   Zuni Fetiches. *2nd Annual Report of the Bureau of American Ethnology*, pp. 2–45. Washington, D.C.

Cushing, Frank Hamilton (*cont.*)

1886   A Study of Pueblo Pottery as Illustrative of Zuni Culture Growth. *4th Annual Report of the Bureau of American Ethnology*, pp. 437−521. Washington, D.C.

1920   Zuni Breadstuff. *Indian Notes and Monographs* 8. New York: Museum of the American Indian. (Reprinted in 1974).

Dechert, Peter

1977   Stella Shutiva. *SWAIA Quarterly* 12:1, pp. 2−5.

Dewey-Kofron Gallery

1977   *Pueblo Pottery Exhibition*. Santa Fe.

Dillingham, Rick

1976   Southwestern Indian Potters: Photographs and Interviews. *Studio Potter* 5:1, pp. 29−39.

1977   The Pottery of Acoma Pueblo. *American Indian Art* 2:4, pp. 44−50, 84.

Di Peso, Charles C.

1974   *Casas Grandes: A Fallen Trading Center of the Gran Chichimeca*. 3 vols. Flagstaff: Northland Press.

1977   Casas Grandes Effigy Vessels. *American Indian Art* 2:4, pp. 32-37, 90.

Dittert, Alfred E., Jr., and Fred Plog

1980   *Generations in Clay: Pueblo Pottery of the American Southwest*. Flagstaff: Northland Press.

Douglas, Frederick H.

1930   *Pueblo Indian Pottery Making*. Leaflet No. 6. Denver: Denver Art Museum, Department of Indian Art.

1933   *Modern Pueblo Pottery Types*. Leaflets No. 53−54. Denver: Denver Art Museum, Department of Indian Art.

1935   *Pottery of the Southwestern Tribes*. Leaflets No. 69−70. Denver: Denver Art Museum, Department of Indian Art.

Dozier, Thomas S.

1907   About Indian Pottery. *Statement to the Trade for 1907*. Santa Fe.

Farrington, William

1975   *Prehistoric and Historic Pottery of the Southwest: A Bibliography*. Santa Fe: Sunstone Press.

Fewkes, Jesse Walter

1898   An Ancient Human Effigy Vase from Arizona. *American Anthropologist* 11:10, pp. 165−170.

1901   Archaeological Expedition to Arizona in 1895. *15th Annual Report of the Bureau of American Ethnology*, Washington, D.C., pp. 245−313.

1904   Two Summers' Work in Pueblo Ruins. *22nd Annual Report of the Bureau of American Ethnology*, pp. 3−195. Washington, D.C.

1909   Ancient Zuni Pottery. In *Putnam Anniversary Volume*. New York: G. E. Stechert and Co., pp. 43−82.

1911   Antiquities of the Mesa Verde National Park: Cliff Palace. *Bulletin of the Bureau of American Ethnology, No. 51*. Washington, D.C.

1916   Animal Figures on Prehistoric Pottery from Mimbres Valley, New Mexico. *American Anthropologist* (n.s.) 18:4, pp. 535–545.

1919   Designs on Prehistoric Hopi Pottery. *23rd Annual Report of the Bureau of American Ethnology*, pp. 207–284. Washington, D.C.

1923   Designs on Prehistoric Pottery from Mimbres Valley, New Mexico. *Smithsonian Miscellaneous Collections* 74:6. Washington, D.C.

Frank, Larry, and Francis H. Harlow

1974   *Historic Pottery of the Pueblo Indian, 1600–1880.* Boston: New York Graphic Society.

Frisbie, Theodore R.

1973   The Influence of J. Walter Fewkes on Nampeyo: Fact or Fancy? *In* Albert H. Schroeder, ed., *The Changing Ways of Southwestern Indians: A Historic Perspective.* Glorieta: The Rio Grande Press, pp. 231–243.

Gifford, E. W.

1978   Pottery Making in the Southwest. *Publications in American Archaeology and Ethnology*, vol. 23. Berkeley: University of California, pp. 353–373.

Gill, Robert R.

1976   Ceramic Arts and Acculturation at Laguna. *In* Nelson H. H. Graburn, ed., *Ethnic and Tourist Arts*. Berkeley: University of California Press, pp. 102–113.

Goddard, Pliny Earle

1931   *Pottery of the Southwestern Indians.* New York: The American Museum of Natural History.

Gratz, Kathleen

1976   Origins of the Tesuque Rain God. *El Palacio* 82:3, pp. 3–8.

Guthe, Carl E.

1925   Pueblo Pottery Making. *Papers of the Southwestern Expedition*, No. 2. New Haven: published for Phillips Academy by Yale University Press.

Halseth, Odd S.

1926   The Revival of Pueblo Pottery Making. *El Palacio* 21:6, pp. 135–154.

Hammack, Laurens C.

1974   Effigy Vessels in the Prehistoric American Southwest. *Arizona Highways* 50:2, pp. 33–34.

Hardin, Margaret Ann

1983   *Gifts of Mother Earth: Ceramics in the Zuni Tradition.* Phoenix: The Heard Museum.

Harlow, Francis H.

1965   Tewa Indian Ceremonial Pottery. *El Palacio* 72:4, pp. 13–23.

1967   *Historic Pueblo Indian Pottery.* Los Alamos: The Monitor Press.

1973   *Matte-paint Pottery of the Tewa, Keres, and Zuni Pueblos.* Santa Fe: Museum of New Mexico.

1977   *Modern Pueblo Pottery, 1880–1960.* Flagstaff: Northland Press.

Harlow, Francis H., and John V. Young
  1965   *Contemporary Pueblo Indian Pottery.* Santa Fe: Museum of New
          Mexico Press.
Hartley, Marsden
  1922   The Scientific Esthetic of the Redman. *Art and Archaeology* 13:3,
          pp. 213–219.
Haury, Emil
  1937   Figurines and Miscellaneous Clay Objects. *In* H. S. Gladwin et al.,
          Excavations at Snaketown: Material Culture. *Medallion Papers,*
          No. 25. Tucson: The University of Arizona Press, pp. 233–245.
  1978   *The Hohokam, Desert Farmers and Craftsmen: Excavations at
          Snaketown, 1964–1965.* Tucson: The University of Arizona Press.
Hodge, F. W.
  1924   Pottery of Hawikuh. *Indian Notes* 1:1, pp. 8–15.
  1942   A Prehistoric Hitler? *Masterkey* 16:6, pp. 220–221.
Holmes, William H.
  1886a   Pottery of the Ancient Pueblos. *4th Annual Report of the Bureau of
          American Ethnology*, pp. 257–360. Washington, D.C.
  1886b   Origin and Development of Form and Ornament in Ceramic Art.
          4th Annual Report of the Bureau of American Ethnology, pp.
          437–465. Washington, D.C.
  1889   The Debasement of Pueblo Art. *American Anthropologist* (n.s.) 2,
          p. 320.
Houlihan, Patrick T., ed.
  1974   Southwestern Pottery Today. Special Edition of *Arizona Highways*
          50:5.
Howard, Richard M.
  1975   Contemporary Pueblo Indian Pottery. In *Ray Manley's Southwest-
          ern Indian Arts and Crafts.* Tucson: Ray Manley Photography, Inc.,
          pp. 32–52.
Jacka, Jerry, and Spencer Gill
  1976   *Pottery Treasures.* Portland: Graphic Arts Center Publishing.
Jeancon, Jean A.
  1931   *Santa Clara and San Juan Pottery.* Leaflet No. 35. Denver: Denver
          Art Museum.
Jeancon, Jean A., and Frederic H. Douglas
  1932   *Hopi Indian Pottery.* Leaflet No. 47. Denver: Denver Art Museum.
Judd, Neil
  1954   The Material Culture of Pueblo Bonito. *Smithsonian Miscellane-
          ous Collections*, Vol. 124. Washington, D.C.
Kidder, A. V.
  1915   Pottery of the Pajarito Plateau and of Some Adjacent Regions in
          New Mexico. *Memoirs of the American Anthropological Associa-
          tion*, Vol. 2:6, pp. 407–462. Menasha, Wis.
  1924   An Introduction to the Study of Southwestern Archaeology, with a
          Preliminary Account of the Excavations at Pecos. *Papers of the*

Southwestern Expedition, No. 1. New Haven, Conn.: published for the Phillips Academy by Yale University Press.

1931   The Pottery of Pecos, Vol. 1. *Papers of the Southwestern Expedition*, No. 5. New Haven, Conn.: published for Phillips Academy by Yale University Press.

1932   The Artifacts of Pecos. *Papers of the Southwestern Expedition*, No. 6. New Haven, Conn.: published for Phillips Academy by Yale University Press.

Kidder, A. V., and Anna O. Shepard

1936   The Pottery of Pecos, Vol. 2. *Papers of the Southwestern Expedition*, No. 7. New Haven, Conn.: published for Phillips Academy by Yale University Press.

King, Scottie

1981   Gift from the Earth [article about Stella Loretto]. *New Mexico Magazine* 59:1, pp. 22−25.

Kirk, Ruth F.

1943   *Introduction to Zuni Fetishism.* Santa Fe: Papers of the School of American Research.

Klamm, Edward

1983   Photo Essay: The Potter's Art [Ada Suina]. *SWAIA: The Official Indian Market Program*, August 20−21. Santa Fe: Draper Corporation.

Koenig, Seymour, ed.

1976   *Hopi Clay, Hopi Ceremony.* Katonah, New York: The Katonah Gallery.

Lambert, Marjorie F.

1966a   A Unique Kokopelli Jar. *El Palacio* 73:2, pp. 21−25.

1966b   *Pueblo Indian Pottery: Materials, Tools, and Techniques.* Santa Fe: Museum of New Mexico Press.

LeFree, Betty

1975   *Santa Clara Pottery Today.* Albuquerque: University of New Mexico Press.

Littlebird, Harold

1979a   I Talk to "Mother Clay" [Margaret Tafoya]. *The New Mexican* (August 12): Indian Market Supplement, pp. 4, 6.

1979b   Acoma Potter Enjoys Her Work [Stella Shutiva]. *The New Mexican* (August 12): Indian Market Supplement, pp. 12, 14.

1979c   Margaret Tafoya: Guardian of Mother Clay. *SWAIA Quarterly* 14:4, pp. 10−12.

Lister, Robert H., and Florence C.

1978   *Anasazi Pottery.* Albuquerque: University of New Mexico Press.

Love, Marian F.

1981   Helen Cordero's Dolls. *The Santa Fean* 9:11, pp. 17−19.

Lyons, Dennis

1976   Helen Cordero, Famed Indian Potter, Giving to Others. *Arizona AAA Highroads* 21:3, pp. 4−6.

McGraw, Kate
    1981   Evelyn Vigil's Pecos Pottery of the Past. *Artists of the Sun* (Official Indian Market Program, *Santa Fe Reporter*), pp. 91–94.

Marriott, Alice
    1948   *Maria: The Potter of San Ildefonso.* Norman: University of Oklahoma Press.

Maxwell Museum of Anthropology
    1974   *Seven Families in Pueblo Pottery.* Albuquerque: University of New Mexico Press.

Mera, H. P.
    1937   The "Rain Bird," A Study in Pueblo Design. *Memoirs of the Laboratory of Anthropology,* Vol. 2. Santa Fe: Museum of New Mexico.
    1939   Style Trends in Pueblo Pottery, 16th–19th Centuries. *Memoirs of the Laboratory of Anthropology,* Vol. 3. Santa Fe: Museum of New Mexico.
    1945   Negative Painting on Southwestern Pottery. *Southwestern Journal of Anthropology* 1:1, pp. 161–166.

Monthan, Guy, and Doris Monthan
    1975   *Art and Indian Individualists.* Flagstaff: Northland Press.
    1977a   Dextra Quotskuyva Nampeyo. *American Indian Art* 2:4, pp. 58–63.
    1977b   Helen Cordero. *American Indian Art* 2:4, pp. 72–76.
    1979   *Nacimientos.* Flagstaff: Northland Press.

Morris, Earl H.
    1927   The Beginnings of Pottery Making in the San Juan Area: Unfired Prototypes and the Wares of the Earliest Ceramic Period. *Anthropological Papers of the American Museum of Natural History,* Vol. 28, pp. 125–198. New York: American Museum Press.

Morss, Noel
    1954   Clay Figurines of the American Southwest. *Papers of the Peabody Museum* 49:1. Cambridge, Mass.: Peabody Museum Press.

Nequatewa, Edmund
    1939   Miniature Pottery. *Plateau* 12:1, p. 18.

New Mexico Magazine
    1975   *The Indian Arts of New Mexico.* 2 vols. Santa Fe, N.M.

Oppelt, Norman
    1976   Southwestern Pottery: An Annotated Bibliography and List of Types and Wares. *Occasional Publications in Anthropology, Archaeology Series,* No. 7. Greeley: Museum of Anthropology, University of Northern Colorado.

Pepper, George H.
    1906   Human Effigy Vases from Chaco Canyon, New Mexico. *Boas Anniversary Volume.* New York: American Museum Press, pp. 320–324.
    1920   Pueblo Bonito. *Anthropological Papers of the American Museum of Natural History,* Vol. 23. New York: American Museum Press.

Perlman, Barbara H.

1980   "Who's Helen Cordero?" *Arizona Arts and Lifestyle* 2:1, p.19.

Peterson, Ashley

1981   Nora Naranjo-Morse: Working with Enchantment. *Artists of the Sun* (Official Indian Market Program, *Santa Fe Reporter*), pp. 81–82.

Peterson, Susan

1977   *The Living Tradition of Maria Martinez.* Tokyo and New York: Kodansha International Ltd.

Philbrook Art Center

1963   *Indian Pottery of the Southwest, Post-Spanish Period: Clark Field Collection.* Tulsa.

Pilles, Peter J., Jr., and Edward B. Danson

1974   The Prehistoric Pottery of Arizona. *Arizona Highways* 50:2, pp. 2–5, 10–31, 43–45.

Plett, Nicole

1984   Helen Cordero: "Be Good to Them Wherever You Go." (Interview) *ART lines* (August), pp. 8–10.

Plog, Stephen

1980   *Stylistic Variation in Prehistoric Ceramics: Design Analysis in the American Southwest.* New York: Cambridge University Press.

Renaud, E. B.

1934   Prehistoric Female Figurines from Arizona. *El Palacio* 36:1–2, pp. 3–11.

Ritzenthaler, Robert

1979   From Folk Art to Fine Art: The Emergence of the Name Artist Among Southwest Indians. *In* Justine Cordwell, ed., *The Visual Arts: Plastic and Graphic.* The Hague: Mouton, pp. 431–438.

Rodeck, Hugo G.

1976   Mimbres Pottery. *American Indian Art* 4:1, pp. 44–52.

Saunders, Charles Francis

1910   The Ceramic Art of the Pueblo Indians. *International Studio* 41:163, pp. 66–71.

Scott, Stuart D.

1960   Pottery Figurines from Central Arizona. *The Kiva* 26:2, pp. 11–26.

Shepard, Anna O.

1965   *Ceramics for the Archaeologist.* Publication 609. Washington, D.C.: Carnegie Institute of Washington.

Sides, Dorothy Smith

1961   *Decorative Art of the Southwestern Indians.* New York: Dover Publications. Reprint of 1936 edition. Santa Ana: Fine Arts Press.

Smith, Watson, Richard B. Woodbury, and Nathalie F. S. Woodbury

1966   *The Excavation of Hawikuh by Frederick Webb Hodge: Report of the Hendricks-Hodge Expedition, 1917–1923.* New York: Museum of the American Indian.

Snow, David H.
 1973   Some Economic Considerations of Historic Rio Grande Pottery. *In*
         Albert H. Schroeder, ed., *The Changing Ways of Southwestern
         Indians: A Historic Perspective.* Glorieta: The Rio Grande Press,
         Inc., pp. 55–72.
Spinden, Herbert J., ed.
 1931   *Introduction to American Indian Art.* New York: The Exposition of
         Indian Tribal Arts, Inc.
Spivey, Richard L.
 1976   Pottery. *In* Clara Lee Tanner, ed., *Indian Arts and Crafts.* Phoenix:
         Arizona Highways, pp. 100–131.
 1979   *Maria.* Flagstaff: Northland Press.
Stanislawski, Michael B.
 1978   If Pots Were Mortal. *In* Richard A. Gould, ed., *Explorations in
         Ethnoarchaeology.* Albuquerque: University of New Mexico Press,
         pp. 201–227.
Stanislawski, Michael B., and Barbara B. Stanislawski
 1978   Hopi and Hopi-Tewa Ceramic Tradition Networks. *In* Ian Hodder,
         ed., *The Spatial Organization of Culture.* London: Duckworth,
         pp. 61–76.
Stevenson, James
 1883   Illustrated Catalogue of Collections Obtained from the Indians of
         New Mexico and Arizona in 1879. *2nd Annual Report of the
         Bureau of American Ethnology,* pp. 307–422. Washington, D.C.
 1884   Illustrated Catalogue of the Collections Obtained from the Pueblos
         of Zuni, New Mexico, and Walpi, Arizona, in 1881. *3rd Annual
         Report of the Bureau of American Ethnology,* pp. 511–594.
         Washington, D.C.
Switzer, Ronald R.
 1969   An Unusual Late Red Mesa Phase Effigy Pitcher. *Plateau* 42:2,
         pp. 39–45.
Tanner, Clara Lee
 1960   The Influence of the White Man on Southwest Indian Art. *Ethno-
         history* 7:2, pp. 137–150.
 1968   *Southwest Indian Craft Arts.* Tucson: The University of Arizona
         Press.
 1976   *Prehistoric Southwestern Craft Arts.* Tucson: The University of
         Arizona Press.
Toulouse, Betty
 1977   *Pueblo Pottery of the New Mexico Indians: Ever Constant, Ever
         Changing.* Santa Fe: Museum of New Mexico Press.
Wade, Edwin L.
 1980   The Thomas Keam Collection, Hopi Pottery: A New Typology.
         American Indian Art 5:3, pp. 54–61.
Wade, Edwin L., and Lea S. McChesney
 1981   *Historic Hopi Ceramics: The Thomas V. Keam Collection of the*

Peabody Museum of Archaeology and Ethnology, Harvard University. Cambridge, Mass.: Peabody Museum Press.

Walker, Willard, and Lydia Wyckoff, eds.
  1983   *Hopis, Tewas, and the American Road.* Middletown, Conn.: Wesleyan University Press.

Watson, Editha L.
  1932   The Laughing Artists of the Mimbres Valley. *Art and Archaeology* 33:4, pp. 189–193.

Wilson, L. L. W.
  1916   A Prehistoric Anthropomorphic Figure from the Rio Grande Basin. *American Anthropologist* 18:4, pp. 548–551.

Wilson, Olive
  1920   The Survival of an Ancient Art. *Art and Archaeology* 9:1, pp. 24–29.

Wormington, H. M., and Arminta Neal
  1951   *The Story of Pueblo Pottery.* Denver: Museum of Natural History.

II. Pueblo Culture and History
Other Pueblo Arts

Aberle, Sophie D.
  1948   The Pueblo Indians of New Mexico: Their Land, Economy and Civil Organization. *Memoirs of the American Anthropological Association*, No. 70. Menasha, Wis.

Babcock, Barbara A.
  1982   Ritual Undress and the Comedy of Self and Other: Bandelier's *The Delight Makers. In* Jay Ruby, ed., *A Crack in the Mirror.* Philadelphia: University of Pennsylvania Press, pp. 187–203.

  1984   Arrange Me Into Disorder: Fragments and Reflections on Ritual Clowning. *In* John J. MacAloon, ed., *Rite, Drama, Festival, Spectacle.* Philadelphia: ISHI, pp. 102–128.

Bahti, Tom
  1968   *Southwestern Indian Tribes.* Flagstaff: K. C. Publications.

Bandelier, Adolph F.
  1890–   Final Report of Investigations Among the Indians of the South-
  1892   western United States, Carried on Mainly in the Years from 1880 to 1885. 2 volumes. *Papers of the Archaeological Institute of America,* American Series 3 and 4. Cambridge, Mass.

  1890   *The Delight Makers.* New York: Dodd, Mead and Company.

Bandelier, A. F., and Edgar L. Hewett
  1973   *Indians of the Rio Grande Valley.* Albuquerque: University of New Mexico Press.

Benedict, Ruth
    1931   Tales of the Cochiti Indians. *Bulletin of the Bureau of American Ethnology*, No. 98. Washington, D.C.
    1934   *Patterns of Culture.* Boston: Houghton Mifflin.
    1935   Zuni Mythology. 2 volumes. *Columbia University Contributions to Anthropology,* Vol. 21. New York.

Boas, Franz
    1928   Keresan Texts. *Publications of the American Ethnological Society,* Vol. 8. New York.

Bolton, Herbert E., ed.
    1916   *Spanish Exploration in the Southwest, 1542–1706.* New York: Charles Scribner's Sons.

Bunzel, Ruth
    1932   Introduction to Zuni Ceremonialism. *47th Annual Report of the Bureau of American Ethnology,* pp. 467–544. Washington, D.C.

Church, Peggy Pond
    1959   *The House at Otowi Bridge: The Story of Edith Warner and Los Alamos.* Albuquerque: University of New Mexico Press.

Collier, John
    1949   *Patterns and Ceremonials of the Indians of the Southwest.* New York: E. P. Dutton and Co., Inc.

Colton, Harold S.
    1949   *Hopi Kachina Dolls.* Albuquerque: University of New Mexico Press.

Coolidge, Mary Roberts
    1929   *The Rain-Makers: Indians of Arizona and New Mexico.* Boston: Houghton Mifflin Company.

Crane, Leo
    1925   *Indians of the Enchanted Desert.* Boston: Little, Brown, and Company.
    1972   *Desert Drums: The Pueblo Indians of New Mexico, 1540–1928.* Glorieta: The Rio Grande Press, Inc. Reprint of the 1928 edition, Boston: Little, Brown, and Company.

Curtis, Edward S.
    1976   *The North American Indian.* Vol. 16. New York: Johnson Reprint Corporation. Reprint of the 1926 edition, Norwood, Mass.: Plimpton Press.

Cushing, Frank Hamilton
    1896   Outlines of Zuni Creation Myths. *13th Annual Report of the Bureau of American Ethnology,* pp. 321–447. Washington, D.C.

Dockstader, Frederick J.
    1954   *The Katcina and the White Man: A Study of the Influence of White Culture on the Hopi Katcina Cult.* Bloomfield Hills, Mich.: Cranbrook Institute of Science.

Dozier, Edward P.
    1961   Rio Grande Pueblos. *In* Edward H. Spicer, ed., *Perspectives in*

American Indian Culture Change. Chicago: University of Chicago Press, pp. 94–186.

1970   *The Pueblo Indians of North America.* New York: Holt, Rinehart and Winston.

Dumarest, Noël
1918   Notes on Cochiti, New Mexico. *Memoirs of the American Anthropological Association*, No. 23, pp. 135-236. Lancaster, Pa.

Dunn, Dorothy
1968   *American Indian Painting.* Albuquerque: University of New Mexico Press.

Dutton, Bertha P., ed.
1948   *Pocket Handbook: New Mexico Indians.* Santa Fe: New Mexico Association on Indian Affairs.

Eggan, Fred
1950   *Social Organization of the Western Pueblos.* Chicago: University of Chicago Press.

Eickemeyer, Carl, and Lilian W. Eickemeyer
1895   *Among the Pueblo Indians.* New York: The Merriam Company.

Espejo, Antonio
1916   Account of the Journey to the Provinces and Settlements of New Mexico. *In* Herbert E. Bolton, ed., *Spanish Exploration in the Southwest.* New York: Charles Scribner's Sons, pp. 161–195.

Fewkes, Jesse Walter
1894   *Dolls of the Tusayan Indians.* Leiden, The Netherlands: E. J. Brill.

1897   Tusayan Katcinas. *15th Annual Report of the Bureau of American Ethnology*, pp. 245–313. Washington, D.C.

1903   Hopi Katcinas. *21st Annual Report of the Bureau of American Ethnology*, pp. 3–126. Washington, D.C.

1906   Hopi Shrines near the East Mesa, Arizona. *American Anthropologist* (n.s.) 8:3, pp. 369–370.

1910   The Butterfly in Hopi Myth and Ritual. *American Anthropologist* (n.s.) 12:4, pp. 576–594.

Fox, Robin
1967   *The Keresan Bridge.* New York: Humanities Press, Inc.

1973   *Encounter with Anthropology.* New York: Harcourt Brace Jovanovich.

Goddard, Pliny E.
1921   *Indians of the Southwest.* New York: American Museum of Natural History.

Goldfrank, Esther Schiff
1927   The Social and Ceremonial Organization of Cochiti. *Memoirs of the American Anthropological Association*, No. 33. Menasha, Wis.

Haeberlin, H. K.
1916   The Idea of Fertilization in the Culture of the Pueblo Indians. *Memoirs of the American Anthropological Association,* No. 3, pp. 1–55. Lancaster, Pa.

Haury, Emil W., ed.
   1954   Southwest Issue. *American Anthropologist* 56:4.
Hedrich, Basil C., J. Charles Kelley, and Carroll L. Riley
   1974   *The MesoAmerican Southwest: Readings in Archaeology, Ethno-history, and Ethnology.* Carbondale, Illinois: Southern Illinois University Press.
Hewett, Edgar L.
   1938   *Pajarito Plateau and Its Ancient People.* Albuquerque: University of New Mexico Press.
   1943   *Ancient Life in the American Southwest.* New York: Tudor Publishing Co.
Hewett, Edgar L., and Bertha P. Dutton
   1945   *The Pueblo Indian World: Studies on the Natural History of the Rio Grande Valley in Relation to Pueblo Indian Culture.* Albuquerque: University of New Mexico and The School of American Research.
Hieb, Louis A.
   1972   Meaning and Mismeaning: Toward an Understanding of the Ritual Clown. *In* A. Ortiz, ed., *New Perspectives on the Pueblos.* Albuquerque: University of New Mexico Press, pp. 163–195.
Kandarian, Sally M., and Helen Hardin
   1976   Santa Fe Indian Market. *American Indian Art* 4:1, pp. 32-33, 58-59.
Lange, Charles H.
   1968   *Cochiti: A New Mexico Pueblo, Past and Present.* Carbondale, Illinois: Southern Illinois University Press.
Lange, Charles H., and Carroll L. Riley, eds.
   1966   *The Southwestern Journals of Adolph F. Bandelier, 1880–1882.* Albuquerque: The University of New Mexico Press.
   1970   *The Southwestern Journals of Adolph F. Bandelier, 1883–1884.* Albuquerque: The University of New Mexico Press.
Lange, Charles H., Carroll L. Riley, and Elizabeth M. Lange, eds.
   1975   *The Southwestern Journals of Adolph F. Bandelier, 1885–1888.* Albuquerque: The University of New Mexico Press.
Lister, Robert H., and Florence C. Lister
   1983   *Those Who Came Before: Southwestern Archaeology in the National Park System.* Tucson: The University of Arizona Press.
Longacre, William A.
   1970   *Reconstructing Prehistoric Pueblo Societies.* Albuquerque: University of New Mexico Press.
Lummis, Charles F.
   1898   *Some Strange Corners of Our Country.* New York: The Century Co.
   1952   *The Land of Poco Tiempo.* Albuquerque: The University of New Mexico Press. Reprint of 1893 edition, New York: Charles Scribner's Sons.
Mails, Thomas E.
   1983   *The Pueblo Children of the Earth Mother.* 2 vols. Garden City, New York: Doubleday and Company, Inc.

Mead, Margaret, ed.

    1973   *An Anthropologist at Work: Writings of Ruth Benedict.* New York: Equinox Books.

Minge, Ward Alan

    1976   *Acoma: Pueblo in the Sky.* Albuquerque: University of New Mexico Press.

Muench, David, and Donald G. Pike

    1974   *Anasazi: Ancient People of the Rock.* New York: Crown Publishers, Inc.

Ortiz, Alfonso

    1969   *The Tewa World: Space, Time, Being, and Becoming in a Pueblo Society.* Chicago: University of Chicago Press.

    1976   The Dynamics of Pueblo Cultural Survival. Paper presented at American Anthropological Association annual meetings. Washington, D.C.

Ortiz, Alfonso, ed.

    1972   *New Perspectives on the Pueblos.* Albuquerque: University of New Mexico Press.

    1979   *Handbook of North American Indians: Southwest,* Vol. 9. Washington, D.C.: Smithsonian Institution.

Ortiz, Simon J.

    1977   *A Good Journey.* Berkeley: Turtle Island.

Parsons, Elsie Clews

    1918   Nativity Myth at Laguna and Zuni. *Journal of American Folklore* 31:120, pp. 256–263.

    1919   Increase by Magic: A Zuni Pattern. *American Anthropologist* n.s. 21, pp. 279–286.

    1920   Notes on Ceremonialism at Laguna. *Anthropological Papers of the American Museum of Natural History* 19:4, pp. 83–131. New York.

    1929–   Isleta, New Mexico. *47th Annual Report of the Bureau of American*
    1930   *Ethnology,* pp. 193–466. Washington, D.C.

    1933   Hopi and Zuni Ceremonialism. *Memoirs of the American Anthropological Association,* No. 39. Menasha, Wis.

    1939   *Pueblo Indian Religion.* 4 Volumes. Chicago: University of Chicago Press.

Roediger, Virginia More

    1941   *Ceremonial Costumes of the Pueblo Indians.* Berkeley: University of California Press.

Sando, Joe S.

    1976   *The Pueblo Indians.* San Francisco: The Indian Historian Press.

Saunders, Charles Francis

    1973   *The Indians of the Terraced Houses.* Glorieta: The Rio Grande Press, Inc. Reprint of the 1912 edition, New York: Putnam.

Scully, Vincent

    1975   *Pueblo: Mountain, Village, Dance.* New York: Viking Press.

Sebag, Lucien
    1971   *L'invention du monde chez les indiens pueblos.* Paris: François Maspero.

Sedgwick, Mary K. (Rice)
    1926   *Acoma, the Sky City: A Study in Pueblo Indian History and Civilization.* Cambridge: Harvard University Press.

Silko, Leslie Marmon
    1977   *Ceremony.* New York: The Viking Press.
    1980   Running at the Edge of the Rainbow: Laguna Stories and Poems (videotape and transcript). In *Words and Place: Native Literature from the American Southwest.* New York: Clearwater Publishing Co.
    1981a   Language and Literature from a Pueblo Indian Perspective. *In* Leslie A. Fiedler and Houston A. Baker, Jr., eds., *English Literature: Opening Up the Canon.* Baltimore: The Johns Hopkins University Press, pp. 54–72.
    1981b   *Storyteller.* New York: Seaver Books.

Smith, Watson
    1952   Kiva Mural Decorations at Awatovi and Kawaika-a, with a Survey of Other Wall Paintings in the Pueblo Southwest. *Papers of the Peabody Museum,* Vol. 37. Cambridge, Mass.

Starr, Frederick
    1897   New Mexico Trip, September, 1897. Manuscript Diary. Chicago, University of Chicago Library, Archives.
    1899   A Study of the Census of the Pueblo of Cochiti. *Proceedings of Davenport Academy of Sciences* 7, pp. 33–45. Davenport, Iowa.

Stevenson, Matilda Coxe
    1894   The Sia. *11th Annual Report of the Bureau of American Ethnology,* pp. 3–157. Washington, D.C.

Stirling, Matthew
    1942   Origin Myth of Acoma and Other Records. *Bureau of American Ethnology Bulletin*, No. 135. Washington, D.C.

Tanner, Clara Lee
    1973   *Southwest Indian Painting.* Rev. ed. Tucson: University of Arizona Press.

Terrell, John Upton
    1973   *Pueblos, Gods and Spaniards.* New York: Dial Press.

Thompson, Laura
    1945   Logico-Aesthetic Integration in Hopi Culture. *American Anthropologist* 47:4, pp. 540–553.

Underhill, Ruth M.
    1948   Ceremonial Patterns in the Greater Southwest. *American Ethnological Society Monograph,* No. 13. New York: J. J. Agustin Publisher.
    1976   *First Penthouse Dwellers of America.* Santa Fe: William Gannon. Reprint of the 1938 edition, New York: J. J. Agustin.

1979   *Pueblo Crafts.* Palmer Lake, Colorado: The Filter Press. Reprint of the 1944 edition, Washington, D.C.: U.S. Bureau of Indian Affairs.

Wallace, Susan E.

1891   *The Land of the Pueblos.* New York: The Columbian Publishing Co.

White, Leslie A.

1932a   The Acoma Indians. *47th Annual Report of the Bureau of American Ethnology,* pp. 17–192. Washington, D.C.

1932b   The Pueblo of San Felipe. *Memoirs of the American Anthropological Association*, No. 38. Menasha, Wis.

1935   The Pueblo of Santo Domingo. *Memoirs of the American Anthropological Association,* No. 43. Menasha, Wis.

1942   The Pueblo of Santa Ana. *Memoirs of the American Anthropological Association,* No. 60. Menasha, Wis.

1962   The Pueblo of Sia. *Bulletin of the Bureau of American Ethnology,* No. 184. Washington, D.C.

WPA Writers' Program

1940   *New Mexico: A Guide to the Colorful State.* New York: Hastings House.

Wright, Barton

1977   *Hopi Kachinas: The Complete Guide to Collecting Kachina Dolls.* Flagstaff: Northland Press.

1984   Kachina Carvings. *American Indian Art* 9:2, pp. 38–45, 81.

III. American Indian Art, Aesthetic Anthropology, Material Culture Studies, Philosophy and History of Art

Anderson, Richard L.

1979   *Art in Primitive Societies.* Englewood Cliffs, New Jersey: Prentice-Hall, Inc.

Arendt, Hannah

1958   *The Human Condition.* Chicago: University of Chicago Press.

Armstrong, Robert Plant

1971   *The Affecting Presence: An Essay in Humanistic Anthropology.* Urbana, Illinois: University of Illinois Press.

1975   *Wellspring: On the Myth and Source of Culture.* Berkeley: University of California Press.

1981   *The Powers of Presence: Consciousness, Myth, and Affecting Presence.* Philadelphia: University of Pennsylvania Press.

Arnheim, Rudolf

    1966   *Toward a Psychology of Art.* Berkeley: University of California Press.

    1971   *Art and Visual Perception: A Psychology of the Creative Eye.* Berkeley: University of California Press.

Barnett, Homer

    1953   *Innovation: The Basis of Cultural Change.* New York: McGraw-Hill.

Bateson, Gregory

    1972   Style, Grace, and Information in Primitive Art. *In* Bateson, *Steps to an Ecology of Mind.* New York: Ballantine, pp. 128–152.

Biebuyck, Daniel, ed.

    1969   *Tradition and Creativity in Tribal Art.* Berkeley: University of California Press.

Boas, Franz

    1940   Representative Art of Primitive People. *In* Boas, *Race, Language and Culture.* New York: Free Press, pp. 535–540.

    1955   *Primitive Art.* New York: Dover Publications, Inc. Reprint of 1928 edition, Cambridge: Harvard University Press.

Briggs, Charles L.

    1980   *The Wood Carvers of Cordova, New Mexico: Social Dimensions of an Artistic "Revival."* Knoxville: University of Tennessee Press.

Brody, J. J.

    1971   *Indian Painters and White Patrons.* Albuquerque: University of New Mexico Press.

Bunzel, Ruth

    1938   Art. *In* Franz Boas, ed., *General Anthropology.* Boston: D. C. Heath and Co., pp. 535–588.

Charbonnier, G.

    1969   *Conversations with Claude Lévi-Strauss.* London: Jonathan Cape.

Csikszentmihalyi, Mihaly, and Eugene Rochberg-Halton

    1981   *The Meaning of Things: Domestic Symbols and the Self.* Cambridge: Cambridge University Press.

Dawson, Lawrence E., Vera-Mae Frederickson, and Nelson H. H. Graburn

    1974   *Traditions in Transition: Culture Contact and Material Change.* Berkeley: Lowie Museum of Anthropology.

d'Azevedo, Warren L.

    1958   A Structural Approach to Esthetics: Toward a Definition of Art in Anthropology. *American Anthropologist* 60:4, pp. 702–714.

d'Azevedo, Warren L., ed.

    1973   *The Traditional Artist in African Society.* Bloomington: Indiana University Press.

Dewey, John

    1934   *Art as Experience.* New York: Capricorn Books.

Dockstader, Frederick J.

    1961   *Indian Art in America: The Arts and Crafts of the North American Indian.* Greenwich: New York Graphic Society.

Dockstader, Frederick J., ed.
   1959   *Directions in Indian Art.* Tucson: The University of Arizona Press.
Douglas, Frederic H., and René D'Harnoncourt
   1941   *Indian Art of the United States.* New York: Museum of Modern Art.
Duvignaud, Jean
   1972   *The Sociology of Art.* Translated by Timothy Wilson. New York: Harper and Row.
Feder, Norman
   1972   *Two Hundred Years of North American Indian Art.* New York: Praeger.
Feest, Christian F.
   1980   *Native Arts of North America.* New York: Oxford University Press.
Firth, Raymond
   1936   *Art and Life in New Guinea.* London: The Studio, Limited.
   1963   *Elements of Social Organization.* Boston: Beacon Press.
Focillon, Henri
   1948   *The Life of Forms in Art.* New York: Wittenborn, Schultz, Inc.
Forge, Anthony, ed.
   1973   *Primitive Art and Society.* London: Oxford University Press.
Geertz, Clifford
   1976   Art as a Cultural System. *Modern Language Notes* 91:6, pp. 1473–1499.
Gerbrands, A. A.
   1957   *Art as an Element of Culture, Especially in Negro-Africa.* Leiden, The Netherlands: E. J. Brill.
   1967   *Wow-Ipits: Eight Asmat Woodcarvers in New Guinea.* The Hague: Mouton.
Girard, Alexander
   1968   *The Magic of a People.* New York: The Viking Press.
Glassie, Henry
   1973   Structure and Function, Folklore and the Artifact. *Semiotica* 7:4, pp. 313–351.
Gould, Richard A., ed.
   1978   *Explorations in Ethnoarchaeology.* Albuquerque: University of New Mexico Press.
Graburn, Nelson H. H., ed.
   1976   *Ethnic and Tourist Arts.* Berkeley: University of California Press.
Greenhalgh, Michael, and Vincent Megaw, eds.
   1978   *Art in Society: Studies in Style, Culture and Aesthetics.* New York: St. Martin's Press.
Haselberger, Herta
   1961   Method of Studying Ethnological Art. *Current Anthropology* 2, pp. 341–355.
Heidigger, Martin
   1967   *What is a Thing?* Chicago: Henry Regnery Co.
   1971   *Poetry, Language, Thought.* New York: Harper and Row.

Helm, June, ed.
  1967   *Essays on the Verbal and Visual Arts.* Seattle: University of Wash-
          ington Press.
Hodder, Ian
  1982   *Symbols in Action: Ethnoarchaeological Studies of Material Cul-
          ture.* Cambridge: Cambridge University Press.
Hodder, Ian, ed.
  1978   *The Spatial Organization of Culture.* London: Duckworth.
Hofstadter, Albert
  1969   On Consciousness and the Language of Art. *In* James M. Edie, ed.,
          New Essays in Phenomenology. Chicago: Quadrangle Books,
          pp. 83–99.
Holm, Bill, and Bill Reid
  1975   *Form and Freedom: A Dialogue on Northwest Coast Indian Art.*
          Houston, Texas: Rice University Institute for the Arts.
Jones, Michael Owen
  1975   *The Hand Made Object and Its Maker.* Berkeley: University of
          California Press.
Jopling, Carol F., ed.
  1971   *Art and Aesthetics in Primitive Society: A Critical Anthology.* New
          York: E. P. Dutton and Co.
Kandinsky, Wassily
  1977   *Concerning the Spiritual in Art.* New York: Dover.
Kaplan, Flora S.
  1981   The "Meaning" of Pottery. *In* Cantwell, Griffin, and Rothschild,
          eds., The Research Potential of Anthropological Museum Collec-
          tions. *Annals of the New York Academy of Sciences,* Vol. 376, pp.
          315–323. New York: The New York Academy of Sciences.
Kempton, Willett
  1981   *The Folk Classification of Ceramics: A Study of Cognitive Pro-
          totypes.* New York: Academic Press.
Kubler, George
  1962   *The Shape of Time.* New Haven: Yale University Press.
Layton, Robert
  1981   *The Anthropology of Art.* London: Granada Publishing.
Leach, Edmund R.
  1956   Aesthetics. *In* E. E. Evans-Pritchard et al. *The Institutions of Primi-
          tive Society.* Oxford: Basil Blackwell, pp. 25–38.
Longacre, William
  1981   Kalinga Pottery: An Ethnoarchaeological Study. *In* I. Hodder, G.
          Isaac, and N. Hammond, eds., *Pattern of the Past: Studies in
          Honor of David Clarke.* Cambridge: Cambridge University Press,
          pp. 49–66.
Maquet, Jacques
  1971   *Introduction to Aesthetic Anthropology.* Reading, Mass.: Addi-
          son-Wesley.

Matson, Frederick R.
   1965   *Ceramics and Man.* Viking Fund Publications in Anthropology, No. 41. New York: Wenner-Gren Foundation.
Merleau-Ponty, Maurice
   1964   *The Primacy of Perception and Other Essays.* Edited by James M. Edie. Evanston: Northwestern University Press.
Mitchell, W. J. T., ed.
   1980   *The Language of Images.* Chicago: The University of Chicago Press.
O'Neale, Lila M.
   1932   Yorok-Karok Basket Weavers. *University of California Publications in Archaeology and Ethnology* 32:1, pp. 1–184. Berkeley.
Otten, Charlotte M., ed.
   1971   *Anthropology and Art: Readings in Cross-Cultural Aesthetics.* Garden City, New York: The Natural History Press.
Panofsky, Erwin
   1982   *Meaning in the Visual Arts.* Chicago: The University of Chicago Press.
Parezo, Nancy J.
   1983   *Navajo Sandpainting: From Religious Act to Commercial Art.* Tucson: The University of Arizona Press.
Paz, Octavio
   1974   Use and Contemplation. In *In Praise of Hands: Contemporary Crafts of the World.* Greenwich: New York Graphic Society, pp. 17–24.
Reina, Ruben E., and Robert M. Hill II
   1978   *The Traditional Pottery of Guatemala.* Austin: The University of Texas Press.
Richardson, Miles, ed.
   1974   *The Human Mirror: Material and Spatial Images of Man.* Baton Rouge: Louisiana State University Press.
Ricoeur, Paul
   1983   On Thinking About the Unthinkable. *University of Chicago Magazine* 76:1, pp. 29–31.
Rosenberg, Harold
   1975   Metaphysical Feelings in Modern Art. *Critical Inquiry* 2:2, pp. 217–232.
Schapiro, Meyer
   1953   Style. *In* A. L. Kroeber, ed., *Anthropology Today.* Chicago: University of Chicago Press, pp. 287–312.
Schrader, Robert Fay
   1983   *The Indian Arts and Crafts Board: An Aspect of New Deal Indian Policy.* Albuquerque: University of New Mexico Press.
Shiff, Richard
   1979   Art and Life: A Metaphoric Relationship. *In* Sheldon Sacks, ed., *On Metaphor.* Chicago: University of Chicago Press, pp. 105–120.

Shils, Edward
1981   *Tradition.* Chicago: University of Chicago Press.
Silver, Harry R.
1979   Ethnoart. *Annual Review of Anthropology* 8, pp. 267–307.
Smith, Marian W., ed.
1961   *The Artist in Tribal Society.* New York: Free Press.
Spinden, Herbert J., ed.
1931   *Introduction to American Indian Art.* New York: The Exposition of
        Indian Tribal Art, Inc.
Taylor, Donna
1959   Anthropologists on Art. *In* Morton H. Fried, ed., *Readings in
        Anthropology,* Vol. 2. New York: Thomas Y. Crowell Company,
        pp. 478–490.
Turner, Victor W., ed.
1982   *Celebration: Studies in Festivity and Ritual.* Washington, D.C.:
        Smithsonian Institution Press.
Ucko, Peter J., ed.
1977   *Form in Indigenous Art: Schematization in the Art of Aboriginal
        Australia and Prehistoric Europe.* Atlantic Highlands, N.J.: Hu-
        manities Press.
Vaillant, George C.
1939   *Indian Arts in North America.* New York: Harper and Brothers.
Weiner, Annette
1980   Reproduction: A Replacement for Reciprocity. *American Ethnol-
        ogist* 7:1, pp. 71–85.
1982   Sticks and Stones, Threads and Bones: This Is What Kinship Is
        Made Of. Paper presented at the Conference on Feminism and
        Kinship Theory, Bellagio, Italy.
Weltfish, Gene
1953   *The Origins of Art.* Indianapolis: The Bobbs-Merrill Company.
1960   The Anthropologist and the Question of the Fifth Dimension. *In*
        Stanley Diamond, ed., *Culture in History: Essays in Honor of Paul
        Radin.* New York: Columbia University Press, pp. 160–179.
Witherspoon, Gary
1977   *Language and Art in the Navajo Universe.* Ann Arbor: University of
        Michigan Press.
Wobst, H. Martin
1977   Stylistic Behavior and Information Exchange. *In* Charles E. Cle-
        land, ed., For the Director: Research Essays in Honor of James B.
        Griffin. *Anthropological Papers*, No. 61. Ann Arbor: University of
        Michigan Museum of Anthropology, pp. 317–342.
Woolf, Janet
1975   *Hermeneutic Philosophy and the Sociology of Art.* London: Rout-
        ledge and Kegan Paul.

Index

Names in *italics* refer to pottery figures. Page numbers in *italics* refer to photographs. Page numbers in **bold** indicate statement by artist.

Designed by Harrison Shaffer
Composed by Typecraft
Color plates printed by Isbell Printing Co.
Printed and bound by Braun-Brumfield, Inc.